why not now?

you don't have to "grow up" to follow jesus

mark matlock

and christopher lyon

why not now?

you don't have to "grow up" to follow jesus

mark matlock
and christopher lyon

six sessions

youth
specialties

ZONDERVAN.com/
AUTHORTRACKER
follow your favorite authors

ZONDERVAN

Why Not Now? Leader's Guide
Copyright © 2012 by Mark Matlock

YS Youth Specialties is a trademark of YOUTHWORKS!, INCORPORATED and is registered with the United States Patent and Trademark Office.

This title is also available as a Zondervan ebook. Visit www.zondervan.com/ebooks.

Requests for information should be addressed to:

Zondervan, *Grand Rapids, Michigan 49530*

ISBN 978-0-310-89263-2

Cover design: Micah Kandros
Interior design: David Conn

Printed in the United States of America

12 13 14 /DCI/ 20 19 18 17 16 15 14 13 12 11 10 9 8 7 6 5 4 3 2 1

For all the students who have set such a great example
for us of what it means to follow Jesus.

contents

miriam
risk bigger

How to Use the DVD

This curriculum package includes a DVD. On it, you'll find Mark presenting the main teaching points for each session. You could make use of this in one of three ways:

1. Play the DVD for your group. This could be effective if your students know Mark or if you don't have a qualified teacher available for your group. It could also be helpful to use the DVD if your group chooses to break up into smaller groups during the teaching time. Another idea would be to watch the video together and then go back through the main points of the teaching more conversationally, using the leader's guide for reference. (Note: The DVD doesn't cover the discussion questions, activities, or other interactive material in this leader's guide.)

2. Use Mark's teaching as part of your preparation. Notice what he emphasizes and how he delivers the content.

3. Skip it! You don't need the DVD to make full use of the curriculum. It's included as a possible enhancement for those who wish to use it.

Introduction

Big moments matter. Sometimes we get only a few seconds to decide how we'll respond when the heat is on. Will we play it safe or take a risk? Will we hang back, or will we put ourselves in the middle of something dangerous, something unfamiliar, something important?

Your students aren't too young to take risks—even significant ones. In fact, some parents see their job (and maybe yours) as convincing their teenagers to take fewer risks—to avoid such things as driving too fast, drinking, and having unmarried sex. It's likely we've all made the argument to students that the risks that come with those behaviors aren't worth the rewards, especially in the long run.

Because of this, it might be difficult to get behind the message that students need to take more and bigger risks in their lives. If you see your role as a lifeguard in your students' teen experience, you're more likely to focus on their safety and stability than on pushing them into difficult—and potentially dangerous—scenarios.

There are two problems with that approach: One, it can never work. Teens take risks. It's part of their developmental process. It's what gives them the courage and momentum to make new friends, leave home, strike out into the world, and choose a life path. They need that risk-taking instinct.

The second problem with the lifeguard strategy is that you're already asking your students to do one of the riskiest things in this life: You're asking them to follow Jesus. You want them to set their course by him—to start using that desire for risk to take off after him, no matter the danger. Jesus' disciples must take the right risks in the right moments if they're going to use their lives most effectively for him.

You want to help your students value risky choices not because of the thrill or a sense of rebelliousness, but because it's an opportunity to be used by God in a way that'll matter for eternity. It takes grown-up wisdom for a teenager to make those choices—your students are capable of it right now.

Are you ready to help them see that?

What's the Story?

It's easier to discover meaningful truth in the context of a good story.

The main story for this session comes from the life of Miriam, Moses' older sister. Concerned for the life of her baby brother, she made a risky choice in a dangerous moment. Because of the risk Miriam took, God saved Moses and, eventually, a whole nation.

In this session you'll also share some supporting stories. One is about one of Moses' own risky choices, and the other is a closing story about a heat-of-the-moment, high-risk decision made by a sixteen-year-old cheerleader in her local mall.

What's the Point?

The goal of this Bible study session is to accomplish two big things:

1. To help your students think biblically about when it's wise to take risks and when it isn't
2. To help your students see themselves as people willing and responsible to take risks for good and for God's glory

What You'll Need

Paper

Pens or pencils

Bibles

Activity

Personality Quiz: Are You a Risk Taker?

Hand out paper and pens or pencils. Ask your students to write down their answers to the following questions from an informal personality quiz. Explain that they won't be asked to share their answers with anyone, so they can be honest with themselves.

1. You're hanging out with a group of people you don't know that well. Someone mentions something that reminds you of a great story you just heard. The conversation lulls for a second. What do you do?

   A. Nothing. Why risk embarrassing yourself in front of people you don't really know?
   B. Decide to tell the story to a good friend later that day.
   C. Whisper the story to someone standing close to you.
   D. Blurt out the story for all to hear and enjoy.

2. You're at a new amusement park with three other friends when someone suggests you all get in line for the Unlunchenator, the biggest roller coaster in the tri-state area.

    A. You immediately fake an ankle sprain and say you'll have to sit this one out.

    B. You politely but firmly explain that you don't trust those things.

    C. You agree to go only if everyone else will and you don't have to sit in the front.

    D. You're already in line.

3. It's your day to give your book report in English class; the teacher asks who wants to go first.

    A. You sit lower in your desk and try to avoid eye contact.

    B. You encourage someone else to go first so you can review your notes for the twentieth time.

    C. You'd rather not go first, but you kind of want to get it over with, so you volunteer.

    D. You jump out of your seat and do a little dance all the way to the front of the room.

4. You go out with your family to a restaurant you like, and your dad points out some new menu items you've never heard of. He decides to try one and suggests everyone get something new this time.

    A. You say, "No way! I want the usual, and I always will."

    B. You're tempted, but you're afraid you might not like it as much as what you usually get. So you agree to try bites of everyone else's.

    C. You get your usual meal, but you order something different on the side.

    D. You get the dish that's the most difficult for you to pronounce.

5. A good friend tells you that her parents have forbidden her from hanging out with the guy she likes. She's way into him,

but you've noticed that he treats her badly, she's started skipping classes with him, and she's sneaking out late at night. You think she should get away from him. What do you say?

A. You agree that parents can sometimes be a real pain and change the subject.
B. You nod sympathetically, but you don't say anything.
C. You kind of ask her if she's sure that being with this guy is what she wants.
D. You tell her that you think she's making foolish choices with this guy and she should listen to her parents.

When everyone's written down his or her choices for each question, instruct your students to give themselves one point for each A choice, two points for each B choice, three points for each C choice, and four points for each D choice. Then have them tally up their scores. Explain what your very unscientific survey says about their tendency to take risks:

Score: 5–9
Risk Skipper
You don't like taking too many risks. You'd rather be safe than sorry. For you, the possible cost of losing deters you from taking a chance to make a big splash.

Score: 10–14
Risk Dabbler
Sometimes you take risks, but only if you're pretty sure you've got a good shot at succeeding . . . or if the payoff for the risk is really exciting.

Score: 15–20
Risk Hugger
You love to take big risks. You're not so worried about what you'll lose if it doesn't pay off. You're more interested in what you'll miss out on if you don't do the scarier thing. Risk is your middle name.

Group Discussion
Worth the Risk?
Get your group talking about risk taking by asking some of the following questions. Encourage everyone to participate, even if some students seem reluctant. Don't shy away from a little debate.

> **Did you agree with your score? Do you think of yourself as a risk taker, or are you someone who prefers to play it safe?**
>
> **Is it right or wrong to take a risk? Or does it depend on the situation?**
>
> **What are some examples of risks that probably aren't worth taking? What are some risks that most people should take?**
>
> **Big question: How can you tell the difference between a risk worth taking and one that you should definitely skip?**

Bible Study
Backstory
Explain to your students the following in your own words:

Our Bible study today will be about taking risks. Specifically, we're going to talk about why we should all be better risk takers who know when to skip a risk and when to take way bigger risks.

Emphasize the following:

Many Christians think that following Jesus means we should always play it safe. Too many of us define being a "good" Christian by all of the things that we don't do. We think of Christians as people who don't drink too much, don't have unmarried sex, don't skip church, don't tell lies, and don't disobey their parents.

And while we *should* avoid those things, following Jesus isn't about where we don't go. It's about where we *do* go. And following Jesus isn't safe—it's risky.

Ask your students to open their Bibles to Exodus 1. Explain the following in your own words:

Miriam was a girl who lived in dangerous times. Her people, the Israelites, were slaves in Egypt. They had been slaves for hundreds

of years. However, the Egyptians were afraid of the Israelites because there were so many of them and they were very strong. So the Egyptians worked them harder and harder to keep them from having the energy to rebel.

Eventually, the Egyptians got so worried about the Israelites that they took drastic action.

Read Exodus 1:15-22 out loud to your group. Explain the following:

The boys born during this time in Israel's history were in serious danger—the government wanted them dead.

Miriam was safe because she was a girl. She had a brother named Aaron who'd already survived. But her mother was about to have another baby. Everyone knew that if the baby was a boy, he'd likely be killed.

Scripture: Exodus 2:1-10

The Big Question: What can we learn from Miriam's story to help us risk bigger?

1. Whose Family Do You Belong To?

Ask a student to read Exodus 2:1-4 out loud to the group. Emphasize the following in your own words:

The situation was so desperate that Moses' mom and dad had to raise their baby in secret for three months, and then they had to do something with him before the government could come and kill him. But there was nowhere to hide him. In what must have been a terrible moment, they tucked him into a floating basket and set it loose on the river, hoping he'd somehow be okay.

But his big sister followed the basket. She refused to let him simply disappear.

This passage doesn't tell us this girl's name, but we find out later in the story of Exodus that she was Miriam. Her brother Moses grew to become the leader of Israel. And Moses' brother Aaron and sister Miriam became known as a prophet and prophetess. They spent their lives together taking care of the Israelites. And that all started in that moment when Miriam made a risky choice.

The first thing we see about Miriam is that she knew what family she belonged to. She saw herself as a child of her parents and a big sister to this little baby. Because they were in the same family, she understood that it was normal for her to be responsible for helping her mom and her brother.

We take good or bad risks, in part, because of what we believe about where we belong in life. People who take dangerous risks with drugs, premarital sex, or drinking have often decided that they're not sure the family they belong to is trustworthy or even worth obeying—or they've decided that they want to belong to a new "family" of friends who like to take those kinds of risks.

As Jesus' followers we know in our heads and hearts that we belong to the family of God. He's adopted us as his sons and daughters. When we're committed to that family, we begin to see ourselves as people who're responsible to God for each other.

Read Galatians 3:26 out loud to your students:

So in Christ Jesus you are all children of God through faith.

People who're convinced that they belong in a family are more ready and willing to take risks for each other.

2. Where's Your Attention?

Ask another student to read Exodus 2:4-6 out loud.

Because Miriam understood what family she belonged to, she felt responsible for her brother. Because she cared about him and her parents, she took the risk to follow the basket in the water to see where it went. If she'd been caught, she could have been killed as well.

People who understand that they're God's children and that they're brothers and sisters to other believers pay attention to the things that God cares about. They look out for each other.

Miriam didn't take her eyes off of that little boat. What are your eyes fixed on?

What we pay attention to has a lot to do with what risky choices we'll face. It's not a sin to be intrigued by sinful things—by things that tempt us to do wrong. But if we keep paying close attention to those things, over and over again we'll be faced with the risky choice to give in to that temptation.

God tells those of us in his family to focus our attention somewhere else.

Read Hebrews 12:1-2 to your students:

> Therefore, since we are surrounded by such a great cloud of witnesses, let us throw off everything that hinders and the sin that so easily entangles. And let us run with perseverance the race marked out for us, fixing our eyes on Jesus, the pioneer and perfecter of faith. For the joy set before him he endured the cross, scorning its shame, and sat down at the right hand of the throne of God.

People in God's family are meant to be paying attention to Jesus.

Hear this, though: When you're paying attention to Jesus and his path, you'll have to make risky choices, choices that could cost you something. In fact, they could cost you dearly. But they'll be choices about taking risks to love your Father and take care of your brothers and sisters in Christ—not taking risks in order to enjoy a few minutes of sin and potentially experience lifelong consequences.

3. What Choice Will You Make?

Ask a third student to read Exodus 2:7-10 out loud to the group.

Because Miriam knew what family she belonged to and because she was paying attention to the right thing, she had to make a risky choice. Would she try to save her brother and help her family, or would she stay quiet because it was too dangerous to talk to the princess of Egypt?

I wonder how long she hesitated before speaking up? I wonder if she thought about not saying anything and just hoping for the best?

Can you remember any moments in your own life when you had to make a quick decision about whether to do a risky thing for someone's good? Do you feel like you made the best choice? How can you know?

These kinds of decisions can be so tough. The Bible says we need God's help to figure them out. What we need is his wisdom. In the heat of the moment, Miriam made a wise choice that saved her baby brother and brought joy to her parents.

Some risks aren't worth the price. The risks that come with sinful choices are *definitely* not worth it. Even if the payoff is great fun or pleasure for a little while, the cost will be great pain for much longer.

Other decisions about risky choices are harder to figure out. A choice made for the right reasons in the wrong moment can lead to disaster. You can certainly do a foolish thing in an effort to serve God. How can you tell if the risk of time, money, safety, or security is what God wants you to do?

We need wisdom. Wisdom is the ability to see life from God's point of view, and we can find it in three different ways: First, we can look for it in the pages of the Bible, especially in the Wisdom Books such as Proverbs and James. Second, we can get it from experience—by taking good and bad risks and learning from our successes and failures. Third, we can ask God for help to make the best possible risky choices.

Read James 1:5 to your students:

If any of you lacks wisdom, you should ask God, who gives generously to all without finding fault, and it will be given to you.

In a few weeks we'll talk about the story of young Solomon asking for a big gift from God, and we'll learn more about getting wisdom.

God seems to have given Miriam wisdom. And courage. Taking the right risks requires both. But you already have everything you need to take those good risks.

Group Discussion

Wise and Risky Choices

Ask your students to talk about some of the following questions:

Can you think of any risky choices you've faced recently where you had to choose whether or not to do something that might cost you something valuable? This choice could be something either good or bad. (These risks could include such things as facing temptation to sin, choosing whether or not to stand up for a friend who was being mistreated, or deciding whether to tell someone about Jesus. Be prepared to talk about risky choices you have faced in your life.)

What are some examples of good risks people take because they love and trust God? (Encourage brainstorming, but be sure to mention some of the following risky choices: serving as a missionary, donating money and time to your church, refusing to go along with friends who want to do wrong, or choosing to say what you believe when you're in a classroom or with a group of people you know will disagree with you.)

Do you think teenagers are too young to take real risks with their time, money, safety, or security as part of following Jesus? (Emphasize that the answer is *no*.)

Do you think that if we make wise and risky choices for God that the result will always come out okay? (Encourage discussion, and then continue to the point below.)

Recap with Moses' Story

Because of Miriam's brave and risky choice, Moses survived and was raised as Egyptian royalty in the palace. But one day he faced a risky choice of his own.

Have a student read Exodus 2:11-15 out loud.

Notice how Moses was motivated to take the risky action he did:

1. **He knew who his real family was.**

   Moses was raised as an Egyptian, but he remembered that he belonged to the family of God. Who's your real family?
2. **He was paying attention to the family of God.**

Because he thought of himself as belonging to God and God's people, Moses was tuned in when he noticed his people being mistreated. What are you paying attention to most: God's business or something else?

3. He made the choice to take risky action.

People might disagree about whether or not Moses should have killed the abusive Egyptian, but Moses acted to protect his family. What would you have done? The next time you face a risky choice to do a good or honorable thing, how will you decide what to do?

Miriam's risky choice led to a happy ending . . . Moses' choice cost him everything he had. He had to run for his life and live in the wilderness. Sometimes, making the right risky choice will lead to great pain. But it might still be the best choice you could possibly make.

Conclusion Story

Wrap up the lesson by telling your students the story of Kealey Oliver, a sixteen-year-old high school cheerleader from Moore, Oklahoma:[1]

In 2010, Kealey was shopping at the local mall and talking on the cell phone with her mom, when she noticed a shoplifter running away from mall security—and straight toward her!

In the heat of the moment, Kealey made a risky choice. Even though she was wearing a strapless dress at the time, she tackled the guy. She saw it as her responsibility as a citizen to stand up for justice.

It cost her some scrapes and bruises, but she also helped to catch a thief.

Was that a wise choice? Was the risk worth the cost? Again, not everyone would agree—including, perhaps, your parents—but it's a great example of someone ready and willing to take risks for what she believes in.

Closing Prayer

Close your session in prayer by asking God to help your students have the courage to make wise and risky choices for him and for those in the family of Christ.

Between Sessions

Do you want to reinforce the main points of this session with your group during the week and prepare them for your next session? Here are a few things you could send out via Facebook, text, Twitter, or email.

Note: Don't send them all. It's helpful to send one the day after your group meets, and then maybe send another a couple of days later. Send teasers for the next session the day before your next meeting.

Session Reinforcement

Remember Miriam: What's God asking you to risk for him this week?

Remember Miriam: Are you focusing on Jesus? Or on what's not working? Risk bigger.

Following Jesus is risky, but it's worth it! Risk bigger.

Next-Session Teasers

How do you fight temptation? Come to group and find out.

Losing to temptation? You don't have to. Come to group and find out how to win!

Join the resistance! This week at group, learn Joseph's secrets to beating temptation.

Of course, these are just starter ideas. Customize these to fit your own group, group name, audience, meeting times, etc.—or just write something way better!

joseph
resist harder

How to Use the DVD

This curriculum package includes a DVD. On it, you'll find Mark presenting the main teaching points for each session. You could make use of this in one of three ways:

1. Play the DVD for your group. This could be effective if your students know Mark or if you don't have a qualified teacher available for your group. It could also be helpful to use the DVD if your group chooses to break up into smaller groups during the teaching time. Another idea would be to watch the video together and then go back through the main points of the teaching more conversationally, using the leader's guide for reference. (Note: The DVD doesn't cover the discussion questions, activities, or other interactive material in this leader's guide.)

2. Use Mark's teaching as part of your preparation. Notice what he emphasizes and how he delivers the content.

3. Skip it! You don't need the DVD to make full use of the curriculum. It's included as a possible enhancement for those who wish to use it.

Introduction

Some of the most important battles we fight take place entirely inside our own heads. These are the grunting, spitting, bleeding, full-contact cage matches between our desires that urge us to do something wrong, easy, pleasurable, or familiar, and God who gently leads us to do something hard—to do the right thing.

It's easy to feel as if talking to teenagers about temptation just doesn't matter—that they will or they won't, no matter what we say. Sometimes the best we can hope for is some uncomfortable silence during the heavy parts of our talk—and we really hope that silence is a sign that they're feeling some conviction. But often that's quickly followed by news that many of them have given in to temptation—sometimes temptation that we also may have indulged in back in the day (or yesterday).

Does it really matter what we say about it?

Of course it does. Our goal isn't to protect teenagers from failing. Our goal is to help them put up a fight—to help them see that they're in a battle. We're to teach them how to be ready to throw up their fists instead of giving in because they see themselves as utterly powerless against their own urges and insecurities. They won't win every round, but we desperately want them to understand that with the power of God's Spirit, every round is winnable and their resistance matters.

Some will fight and lose. Some will win and then lose and then win more often, just as we're learning to do. But this week you can give them some tools to be better fighters. The importance of that job can't be underestimated.

What's the Story?

It's easier to discover meaningful truth in the context of a good story.

The main story for this session is a familiar one. It comes from the life of Joseph. Serving as a slave, Joseph earned a top spot in his master's household and then faced repeated sexual advances from his master's wife. Although your students may know the story well, it still holds excellent insights for how any of us can face and defeat temptation.

In this lesson you'll also share some supporting stories. David's failure to resist temptation when he saw Bathsheba bathing on the roof will make the same point with a negative example. And a recent story about how our brains work will show that teens are more than capable of resisting temptation.

What's the Point?

We hope to accomplish two big things with this Bible study session:

1. To help our students more deeply understand that they're both able and responsible to resist temptation to sin
2. To equip our students with biblical strategies to help them win battles with temptation to sin

What You'll Need

Bibles

Paper

Pens or pencils

Group Discussion

To get your group talking about temptation, start your time by asking them a few questions about common temptations teens (and everybody else) face every day. As always, guide the discussion to help your students arrive at productive answers.

How would you define the word *temptation*?

What's the difference between temptation to do something sinful and temptation to do something that's just foolish? (Some examples of foolish temptations are procrastinating, texting too much, and eating too much junk food.)

What are some of the most common temptations that your friends have to deal with? (Encourage all kinds of examples. The obvious ones might include having sex, drinking alcohol, and disobeying parents. Help them see that we also face temptation to lie, cheat, disrespect people in authority, brag, and be unkind.)

How is facing temptation different for a follower of Jesus than for an unbeliever? Is there a difference? Should there be? (Jesus followers define right and wrong by Jesus' standards. An unbeliever may not see temptation in the same way if they don't agree with the Bible's teaching on good and evil.)

If you think of temptation as a fight, whom are you fighting?
(Help your students to see that though it sometimes feels as if we're fighting against those who're offering us an opportunity to sin, the fight is really with ourselves.)

What are some of the best strategies for resisting temptation to sin? (Let them brainstorm some ideas for a while, and then tell them that you'll be teaching them some specific strategies to help them resist temptation.)

Bible Study

Backstory

Explain to your teens the following in your own words:

In today's Bible study, we're going to talk about how Joseph resisted a terrible temptation when he was about your age. We're going to search his story for some strategies to help us win our own fights with temptation.

You'll be studying the story of Joseph when he was Potiphar's slave. Catch your students up to this point by quickly reminding them of what had previously gone on in Joseph's life:

Joseph was one of twelve brothers. They were all sons of Jacob, and they were the beginning of God's chosen people who would become known as Israel. Joseph's mom was dead, and he was one of his dad's favorite sons. Joseph's brothers hated him because of that and because Joseph told them about his dreams in which they all bowed down to him.

So one day, Joseph's ten older brothers threw him in a hole and used animal blood on his clothes to make it look as if he'd been killed. They sold him to Egyptian slave traders to get rid of him, and then they lied and told their dad that Joseph was dead.

Joseph was purchased by Potiphar, an important man in Egypt.

Scripture: Genesis 39

The Big Question: What strategies can we learn from Joseph's story to help us resist temptation?

Strategy 1: Serve with Everything You've Got—Right Now

Ask a student to read Genesis 39:2-6 out loud to the group. Emphasize the following in your own words:

Think about how you might have felt if you'd been in Joseph's place: Your mom is dead. Your brothers nearly killed you, and then they sold you. Now you're a slave in a foreign country— owned by another person. Basically, your life is ruined. You have little hope of ever being reunited with your dad or the younger brother whom you love.

It would've been easy for Joseph to become an angry, depressed teenager. It would've been easy for Joseph to turn his back on God, even though he'd grown up believing in God. Joseph could've decided, "If my God allows me to suffer like this, he must not be a very good God."

Instead, Joseph kept his hope in God and went to work doing exactly what God gave him to do. For now, that meant serving Potiphar with everything he had. God blessed Joseph's work, and Potiphar noticed, quickly promoting Joseph until he had the top spot in Potiphar's large household.

What does any of this have to do with temptation? The first step in resisting temptation is to have something more important to do instead. Sometimes one of the reasons we so easily give in to temptation to sin is that we don't believe we really have anything to lose. We'll see that Joseph was doing something that mattered, and so he understood that choosing to sin would be very costly.

Read Colossians 3:17 to your students:

And whatever you do, whether in word or deed, do it all in the name of the Lord Jesus, giving thanks to God the Father through him.

You may think that the work you have to do in your life doesn't matter very much right now. You're "just" a student, "just" one of your parents' kids, "just" an employee at a part-time job, "just" a high school athlete, "just" another kid being processed through the system. In fact, you might really resent

your life and think that your "real life" is going to start once you get past where you are now.

That's a lie that makes it easy for us to serve ourselves and give in to temptation.

Christians are told to serve God with everything we've got. Right now. Today. To do it all—school, work, friendship, sports, family—in the name of Jesus, and to thank God for it. Your work matters right now. To God. To those you serve in his name. And, hopefully, to you.

When you believe that, the knowledge that giving in to sin means you'll be sacrificing the work you've been given today makes temptation a lot less attractive.

Strategy 2: Spell Out What It'll Cost and Whom It'll Hurt

Ask another student to read Genesis 39:6-9 out loud.

Now the temptation comes. Potiphar's wife commands Joseph to have sex with her. We don't honestly know if Joseph was even attracted to her, but we're told that he was a handsome, well-built young man. He likely had the same sexual desires any other young guy would have.

Either way, he's facing a real temptation. He might really want to have sex with Mrs. Potiphar. Or he might be tempted to give in to her just to get her to leave him alone. In a way, she's also his boss. He could have easily talked himself into doing what she told him to.

He does just the opposite. He explains to her (and to himself) exactly what he'll lose and whom he'll hurt by doing what she offers: He'll lose all of the gains he's made as a slave. He'll abuse his master's trust in him. And he'll sin against (hurt and offend) God.

Often, we can help ourselves resist temptation to sin by simply slowing down long enough to use the wisdom skill of looking into the future and seeing what the likely outcome will be.

What could it cost us? Who will we hurt? What will likely happen to our key relationships if we get caught?

Strategy 3: Say No—Repeat

Ask a third student to read Genesis 39:10 out loud to the group.

Sometimes we look for ways to resist temptation without actually saying the word *no:* We make an excuse. Shrug it off. Pretend like we didn't hear the offer—from ourselves or someone else. Create a diversion.

The result of this approach is that we leave the door open for the next offer. Joseph said, "No!" It takes courage to say that word—clearly and out loud—but it makes it so much easier to say it the next time the same opportunity to sin comes along.

Strategy 4: Run Away!

Ask someone else to read Genesis 39:11-12 out loud to the group.

The next strategy Joseph models for us is that he didn't just hang out and wait to be tempted. He didn't linger, waiting to passively resist the next opportunity to sin. He tried to take control of the situation in order to keep himself from being forced into having to resist over and over again.

He planned his days so he'd never have to be alone in a room with Mrs. Potiphar. If you're repeatedly tempted to do a specific sin, what can you do to reorganize your life—your schedule, who you spend time with, where you go online or in the real world—to take you out of the path of that opportunity?

Don't be passive. Take the offense in your battle with temptation.

And when Mrs. P brought the fight to Joseph, he was ready to take things up another notch. He ran. He left his cloak behind and ran away from her and toward what was right.

Listen to what Paul wrote in 2 Timothy 2:22—

Flee the evil desires of youth and pursue righteousness, faith, love and peace, along with those who call on the Lord out of a pure heart.

Avoid whenever possible. Flee when necessary. Those are essential strategies in our fight with temptations to sin.

Strategy 5: Expect to Pay a Price

Have someone else read Genesis 39:13-20 aloud. It's a bit longer, so you might pick a good reader or read it yourself.

Giving in to temptation to sin always costs us something. But sometimes, resisting temptation also comes with a price. Joseph probably didn't know how much it would cost him to say no.

Refusing to participate in sin can cost us relationships with people we care about. It can cost us excitement. It can even cost us things we think we need, such as money and time. Choosing not to take an easy way out by doing something sinful (such as telling a lie or cheating on an assignment) can often lead to a much more difficult path to accomplish the same goal.

Does that seem wrong? Do you think that if we make the right choice, God should always reward us with something good?

That's not the way God works on this side of eternity. Those we see in the Bible (and in our own lives) who follow God the closest by resisting temptation and doing good often end up suffering as much—or more than—everyone else.

Here's the weird thing: For many of us, expecting it to cost us something makes it easier to resist temptation instead of harder. It feels more meaningful to do good for God when we know we're making a real sacrifice in doing so. It's when we expect nothing to change that we stop caring about doing the right thing.

Your choices to resist temptation may very well come with a high price tag. Joseph's choice cost him everything—everything except for God's blessing.

Strategy 6: Don't Forget That God Is with You—Right Now

Have one more student read Genesis 39:20-23 out loud.

The end of this chapter reads a lot like the beginning—except now Joseph is in prison. Again, Joseph refused to become angry, depressed, or rebellious. He did exactly what he knew to do: He served God with everything he had right where he was. And God blessed him again—right where he was.

For Joseph, the most important thing was knowing that God was with him all the time—no matter where he ended up or what he ended up doing.

Remembering that God is with us may be the most powerful strategy to resisting temptation to sin. Most often, in fact, to give in to temptation to sin requires giving ourselves a kind of temporary amnesia. We have to make ourselves "forget" that God is right here with us while we're choosing to do the thing we know he hates.

One of the last things Jesus said to his disciples before leaving the planet was this: "Surely I am with you always, to the very end of the age" (Matthew 28:20).

The point isn't that God will "get us" if we do something fun that he doesn't like. Jesus didn't promise to be with us as a threat. His promise to us is that we'll have access to God's power, comfort, strength, hope, and promises because Christ is with us. And those are exactly the things we need when it's time to resist temptation.

Activity
Which Strategy Do You Need to Work On?

Explain to your group that you're going to ask them to participate in a self-assessment quiz where they're to grade themselves on each of these six strategies for resisting temptation to sin. Make sure everyone has a paper and pen or pencil. Encourage them to keep their responses to these questions private so they can be fully honest with themselves and God.

Suggest that as they listen to your questions about each of the six strategies, they give themselves a letter grade for how they've been doing in that area. Then encourage them to write down an idea or two for how they could improve.

Strategy 1: Serve with everything you've got—right now.

Do you see the things you're responsible for in your life as important to God or to you? How much effort do you

put into serving others and God in the things you do at school? At home? At a job? In sports? In your friendships? Do you care about serving with excellence even if nobody else takes it seriously? Does it matter to you that your work gets done right?

Ideas for improvement: **Make a list of your "jobs." For each one, write an idea for how you could do that job better as a service to God. Ask someone you trust to suggest a few ways you could take your responsibilities more seriously.**

Strategy 2: Spell out what it'll cost and whom it'll hurt.

When faced with temptation, do you evaluate what it might cost you? Do you think about the effect your choice might have on other people involved or on your relationship with them? Do you think about how it might hurt God or affect your relationship with him?

Ideas for improvement: **Think about someone you know who got caught giving in to a temptation to sin. Make a quick list of who got hurt and what it cost them. Ask God to make you wise in thinking ahead about the cost of your choices.**

Strategy 3: Say no—repeat.

When faced with temptation, do you just say no? Or do you look for excuses to avoid the wrong choice without having to reject it? Does it get easier for you to say no, or does it get harder when you're faced with the same temptation over and over?

Ideas for improvement: **Make a plan to say the word *no* out loud (even if you're all by yourself) the next time you face a temptation to sin.**

Strategy 4: Run away!

Do you have an active plan to avoid the places, people, or circumstances that make the temptation to sin the most intense for you? When you're "caught" by temptation, do you have the courage not to care about looking cool and to just run away?

Ideas for improvement: **Make a list of a few of the situations in which you face the greatest temptation and think about what it would take to avoid them. Ask a Christian friend you trust what they think you could do to stay away from tempting situations (and really listen to their answers).**

Strategy 5: Expect to pay a price.

Have you thought about what it might cost you if you choose to please God instead of serving your own sinful wants? Have you thought about the time, money, or friendships you might lose by doing the right thing?

Ideas for improvement: **Make a quick list of what you might get or keep by giving in to a specific temptation to sin.**

Strategy 6: Don't forget that God is with you—right now.

How often are you consciously aware that God is with you? How often do you remind yourself of it by praying, reading the Bible, talking about him with other people, or listening to music about him?

Ideas for improvement: **Build habits that force you to be aware of God more than once a day. Memorize Matthew 28:20 and say it to yourself every day for a month.**

Recap with David's Story

The example we've studied from Joseph's life is a positive one. He successfully used six strategies to resist temptation. David's sin with Bathsheba provides a negative example. He didn't use any strategies, and he failed to resist temptation.

Read 2 Samuel 11:1-5 out loud to your students.

In the Bible, David is described as a man after God's own heart. God used this king, whom he loved, to write much Scripture. But when David faced this temptation, he gave in quickly; and then he just kept making it worse with more sinful choices. Notice how he failed to use these strategies:

1. David wasn't serving God with everything he had.

>At this time, David's place was with his army in battle. Instead, he sent the army out without him. He stayed home. He had nothing better to do when temptation came along.

2. **David didn't think about the cost of his sin. He didn't think about who might be hurt.**

   >David was the king. He took what he wanted. He didn't pause to think about the consequences for himself, for Bathsheba, for her husband, or for any child that might be conceived. And he didn't seem to think about what God's response would be.

3. **David didn't say no to himself.**

   >Even kings must take orders from themselves to avoid giving in to temptation.

4. **David didn't make a plan to avoid temptation or run from it.**

   >David saw Bathsheba bathing and he lingered.

5. **David didn't think about what it would cost to tell himself no.**

   >There's a price for resisting temptation. But if we force ourselves to think about it, we're likely to notice how much less expensive it is than caving in.

6. **David chose to "forget" that God was with him.**

   >The man after God's own heart thought he could put God on "pause" long enough to give in to temptation and then be done with it.

If you have time, briefly explain to your teens the consequences of David's choice to give in to temptation. Notice how God used a fictional story—from the prophet Nathan—to finally convict David of his sin. (2 Samuel 11:5–12:23)

Conclusion Story

Wrap up the lesson by telling your group the following:

>There are two stories the world will tell you to try to get you to believe that you can't control yourselves—that teens can't help but to give in to temptation to sin.

The first story goes like this: Because of hormones and developing brains, teenagers just can't say no to some temptations.

But this isn't what the Bible says. God used teenagers over and over to accomplish his missions. He trusted these young people to make right choices—and often they did.

In addition, a study of teenage brains published in the journal *Neuron* in March of 2011 showed that a teenager's ability to resist pressure to make harmful risky choices actually gets stronger during this time of life.[1]

The second story the world will try to tell you (or that you'll try to tell yourself) is that you just can't handle temptation like other people. You, personally, are weaker. You're especially vulnerable to temptation to sin.

Paul calls that bogus in 1 Corinthians 10:13 when he writes, "No temptation has overtaken you except what is common to mankind. And God is faithful; he will not let you be tempted beyond what you can bear. But when you are tempted, he will also provide a way out so that you can endure it."

God says we're not special. Everybody struggles with temptation just as we do. And God provides help to every child of his. There's always a way out. It's never too late.

Closing Prayer

Close your session in prayer by asking God to help your students have the courage to stand up to the temptation to sin, to trust God for a way out, and to use Joseph's strategies to make them stronger in the fight against their own desire to sin. Thank him that victory in his power is always possible.

Between Sessions

Do you want to reinforce the main points of this session with your group during the week and prepare them for your next session? Here are a few things you could send out via Facebook, text, Twitter, or email.

Note: Don't send them all. It's helpful to send one the day after your group meets, and then maybe send another a couple of days later. Send teasers for the next session the day before your next meeting.

Session Reinforcement

What's your strategy to beat temptation this week? Write it down.

You aren't the only one who wants to sin. Read 1 Cor. 10:13.

Resist harder! God always provides a way out. Read 1 Cor. 10:13.

Don't be cool! Leave temptation behind and run away. Be a dork!

Next-Session Teasers

What's the difference between being brave and being stupid? Come to group and find out.

Brave much? You could be. No talent required. Find out more at group.

Feel like following Jesus is too hard for you? Stop whining and get brave. Find out how at group this week.

Ready for the R-rated version of David and Goliath? It's on at group this week.

Of course, these are just starter ideas. Customize these to fit your own group, group name, audience, meeting times, etc.—or just write something way better!

david
believe braver

How to Use the DVD

This curriculum package includes a DVD. On it, you'll find Mark presenting the main teaching points for each session. You could make use of this in one of three ways:

1. Play the DVD for your group. This could be effective if your students know Mark or if you don't have a qualified teacher available for your group. It could also be helpful to use the DVD if your group chooses to break up into smaller groups during the teaching time. Another idea would be to watch the video together and then go back through the main points of the teaching more conversationally, using the leader's guide for reference. (Note: The DVD doesn't cover the discussion questions, activities, or other interactive material in this leader's guide.)

2. Use Mark's teaching as part of your preparation. Notice what he emphasizes and how he delivers the content.

3. Skip it! You don't need the DVD to make full use of the curriculum. It's included as a possible enhancement for those who wish to use it.

Introduction

As youth leaders, we hold up a lot of words that represent qualities we hope our students will aspire to: *purity, wisdom, love, kindness, courage, joy, peace,* and *self-control.* Sometimes we use the word *strength.* But we don't often point to *bravery.*

The word *bravery* comes up when we want small children to stop crying when something hard happens and we tell them to "be brave." We're impressed by the bravery of injured athletes or others who "fight through the pain" to deliver an impressive performance. And, of course, we think of rescue workers and all who fight for us in the armed forces as brave.

But who should be braver than students with a sincere faith in the unconquerable power of God at work in them? This session is all about asking our teens to expect themselves to be brave.

Admittedly, there can be a thin line between bravery and cockiness. We're turned off by sixteen-year-olds full of hubris, buying into the self-aggrandizing swagger of some athletes and hip-hop stars. We don't want that. But the answer isn't to wish for teens who confuse humility with timidity, so fearful of pride and the world that they're unable to step into a spiritual battle and wield the weapons God has given to them.

The antidote to both attitudes—and the key to godly bravery—is faith. Big belief in the power of God and big belief in God's mission for us creates brave people. Our students can and should be brave when acting in the will of God.

Let's tell our teens that.

What's the Story?

It's easier to discover meaningful truth in the context of a good story.

Everyone knows the story of David and Goliath, but very few of us envision it as it's actually described in the Bible.

The images many of us see in our heads when we think about David and his battle with Goliath include adorable and hilarious singing vegetables. Others may picture the Bible art from their Sunday school curriculum or illustrated children's Bibles.

And as appropriate as it may be to edit the version of the story when we tell it to children, we're not talking to children now. David wasn't a child when he fought Goliath. He may have been a teenager, eager to be included in his big brothers' world of war, and completely convinced of the power and rightness of his God.

This is a bloody story featuring a wicked, swearing villain; a battlefield strewn with the bodies of an enemy cut down as they ran for cover; and a brave, faith-filled teenage boy standing before his king holding the still-dripping head of his enemy as a testament to the power of God.

It's the kind of story that should make all of us want to be braver.

In this session you'll also find two supporting stories: You'll read about Paul's bravery as he repeatedly got up every time he was knocked down by those who wanted him to shut up about Jesus. He wouldn't give up, even though he knew his own body was a fragile "jar of clay."

And Abby Sunderland's story of attempting to sail around the world solo when she was sixteen years old can inspire bravery in people of all ages.

What's the Point?

We hope to accomplish two big things with this Bible study session:

1. To help motivate our students to want to do brave things for God
2. To help our students understand that true bravery comes from bigger faith in a powerful, good, and loving God

What You'll Need

A few Ping-Pong balls

A slingshot or other device for launching Ping-Pong balls farther than they can be thrown (see Activity section for alternative ideas)

A small prize for a contest winner (for example: a candy bar, a little trophy, a high-five)

Bibles

Group Discussion

What's Bravery?

Get your group talking about bravery by asking some of the following questions. Encourage participation and storytelling as students talk about what it means to be brave.

How would you define the word *bravery*?

Do you think being brave is just part of your personality or can anyone choose to be brave?

What are some examples of people acting bravely?

Does it matter if we're brave? Do you ever need to be brave in your own everyday world?

What's the difference between being brave and being arrogant and foolish?

Activity

When the Underdog Isn't

With this activity we're hoping to illustrate that bravery for those of us who trust in God comes from having confidence in his power—not in our own.

You'll need a fairly large room or area for this activity, such as a gym, hallway, or even a church sanctuary. Most normal-sized rooms will be too small. (However, you should be able to customize this activity to fit whatever setup you have available.)

In order to pull this off, it'll be very important to test this activity ahead of time. You want to make sure you get the desired result, so a little practice will make a big difference.

Also, you'll need an accomplice: A couple of days ahead of time, explain the activity to the smallest boy or girl in your group. Give that person a chance to practice with you. He or she'll be in on the punch line, but encourage him or her not to tell anyone.

Begin by asking for two volunteers for a contest to see who can get a Ping-Pong ball to go the farthest. Use very specific language. Say, "Who can *get* . . ." not, "Who can *throw* a Ping-Pong ball the farthest."

Choose two contestants: the biggest, strongest guy in your group and the smallest person (the person who is in on the game). Make a big deal of the fact that the smaller student is volunteering. Ask if she *really* expects to have a chance to win. (Encourage her ahead of time to act very confident.) Make a point of saying how brave she's being.

Have both contestants stand next to you and explain that you'll give a prize to the person who can get the ball to go the farthest. Ask the group as a whole to vote for which of the two they think will win.

Start by handing a Ping-Pong ball to the bigger student, and ask him to get the ball as far as he possibly can. Have someone available to mark where the ball lands. Then announce that it's the other student's turn. But before you hand her the Ping-Pong ball, pull from a bag (or some other hiding place) a slingshot, Ping-Pong ball shooter, or other device for propelling Ping-Pong balls a long distance. It should be something that can easily surpass the longest anyone would be able to throw a Ping-Pong ball under normal conditions. (This is why it's important for the student to practice ahead of time.)

Note: Customize this activity to whatever will work for you. If you can do it outside, you could ask who can get water in plastic cups to go the farthest and then secretly give the smaller student a Super Soaker. If you can only be in a small room, you could try it with wadded up pieces of paper and a slingshot. Be creative with the resources and space available to you.

It's important that no matter how you modify this activity, the smaller student should win easily. You can then give her whatever small prize you brought with you.

Hopefully your group will protest. When they do, explain the point of the game: The smaller student was able to be brave in volunteering for a contest she should normally expect to lose because she trusted in an external power source. On her own, she probably would have lost. With the extra power of the slingshot, she knew she could win.

Explain that is very much what it's like to be brave as a Christian. The more confident we are in God's power, the braver we'll be in the heat of the moment. Big belief leads to big bravery.

Bible Study

Backstory

Explain that today you'll be learning about where Christians get their bravery. Deliver the following in your own words:

We'll be looking at a story about David from when he was probably still a teenager. People don't often expect teenagers to be brave, and the people in David's life didn't expect him to be brave. But we shouldn't be surprised when someone who trusts God is brave.

We'll be talking about David's battle with Goliath—but not the little kids' Sunday school version. This is the "R-rated" edition, full of violence and cursing. David wasn't a cute little boy when he killed Goliath—he was a good-looking young guy who stepped up when nobody else would.

We'll be reading together from 1 Samuel 17, but we learn some important things about David in the chapter before that. First, we learn that David had already been chosen by God to be the next king of Israel, even though he was still so young. Second, we learn that he was a talented musician who already worked in the palace playing music for Saul and serving as one of his armor-bearers.

This is what one of Saul's men said about the teenage David when Saul asked who they could find to come and play music for the king: "I have seen a son of Jesse of Bethlehem who knows how to play the lyre. He is a brave man and a warrior. He speaks well and is a fine-looking man. And the LORD is with him." (1 Samuel 16:18)

Apparently, David, though not yet considered a full-grown adult, already had a reputation in his community as a brave man and a warrior (though as far as we know, he had yet to fight in any battles with a human enemy). He was regarded as good-looking and articulate. People understood that God was with him.

Where does bravery come from? You and I might not become kings, but as believers in Jesus we know that God is with us. His Spirit is with us. In a way, we have the same advantage David had. How does that knowledge turn into bravery?

That's what we're going to look for in the awesome story of David and Goliath.

To kick off the story, read 1 Samuel 17:1-11 aloud. Make the point that Goliath was almost ten feet tall, wore impenetrable-seeming armor that weighed one hundred and twenty-five pounds, and carried a thick spear with a spearhead that weighed fifteen pounds. Even the best of Israel's soldiers couldn't have hoped to beat him in a one-on-one battle.

Scripture: 1 Samuel 17
The Big Question: What can we learn from David's story to help us to believe braver?

1. David Was Busy Serving God Right Where He Was
Ask a student to read 1 Samuel 17:12-15 out loud to the group. Emphasize the following in your own words:

David didn't sit around at home waiting for his big moment to come. He made himself available to God right where he was—he did whatever God asked of him. He didn't say to himself, "When I get out on my own, I'll get serious about serving God." He started at home, serving God and his family by tending sheep.

He also served God by serving his king. David worked part-time at the castle playing music to help Saul and performing other duties as an armor-bearer.

Bravery isn't something that happens in a flash when a need arises—God empowers available people to do brave things when he needs them done. If you want to do brave things for God, you must start by being available to him for ordinary things that need to be done today.

2. David Obeyed His Dad
Ask another student to read 1 Samuel 17:17-24 out loud.

Not only was David busy serving God right where he was, he also obeyed his father. David could have had a different attitude. He could have said, "I've been anointed as the next king of Israel, and I serve in the palace. I don't think I should have to run your errands anymore, Dad. Let one of the servants do it." But instead, David obeyed. And did you notice where his

obedience took him? He arrived at the battle right when Goliath stepped out to challenge and mock the Israelites.

God directs our lives through those in authority over us. If David hadn't obeyed his dad, there never would have been the story of David and Goliath. People who trust God obey him (and their parents—because God tells them to). And people who trust God grow brave. God uses obedience—even to mundane, everyday things—to put his brave people in the right place at the right time.

3. David Asked Good Questions

Ask a third student to read 1 Samuel 17:25-27 out loud to the group.

We tend to think of bravery as a quick decision to do something heroic without stopping to think about it. Brave people take action first and ask questions later, right?

Sometimes. However, brave action more often occurs after there's time to think it through. In fact, to act without thinking when you don't have to make a decision in the moment isn't brave—it's foolish. David took the time to make sure he understood exactly who Goliath was, as well as the risks and possible rewards for the one who stood up to the giant.

It's true that bravery often requires a person to act even when it seems as if success would be unlikely without God's help. But making those decisions also requires wisdom. David wisely asked questions.

We can, too.

4. David Ignored Those Who Said He Was Too Young

Have someone read 1 Samuel 17:28-33 to the group.

It's a classic sibling moment. David's oldest brother sounds like oldest brothers (or sisters) everywhere and in every time. He questions David's motives for wanting to know about Goliath and wanting to help in the battle. He's angry that his littlest brother is getting in the way.

Sometimes those closest to us will try to talk us out of acting bravely in God's power and for God's purposes. It makes sense that our families and the friends we grew up with might have trouble seeing us as anything other than that "little kid" they've always known. They might be nicer about it than David's brother, but they still leave the impression that we should leave the big jobs for other people.

David ignored his brother.

Then the king told David the same thing: "You're too young. He's too big, too strong, and too experienced."

Every parent I know would have agreed with Saul had it been their son eager to go into battle with a giant. And they would have been wrong. David was right to say what he said next to the king. (Note, however, that David did not disobey his parents. His dad wasn't there to say David was too young. If he had been, David would have been wrong to defy him. God directs us through those in authority. See point #2.)

Sometimes the hardest part of being brave in God's power and for his purposes is respectfully ignoring the voices trying to talk you out of it.

5. David Trusted God's Proven Power

Another reader can take the group through 1 Samuel 17:34-40.

Goliath was a proven warrior. He'd probably killed many men in battle. David had never fought in a military battle in his life—he didn't know what he was getting himself into.

As impressive as it was that he'd killed a bear and a lion (and that's pretty impressive), it's not the same as killing a battle-hardened warrior whose armor and weapons probably weigh more than you do. And David wasn't claiming it was the same. He was saying that he had experience being rescued by God— that he had power that came from outside of himself. That's something Goliath couldn't claim.

And that's where David's bravery came from: The God who has saved me before can do it again. I fight for him, and I trust him. If he fights through me, the giant doesn't have a chance.

That's where our bravery should come from, too. If we're called on to do a brave thing for God, we can be completely confident that he'll give us all of the power we need in order to do it. The more we believe that, the braver we'll be.

6. David Boasted Only in God's Power

Have someone read 1 Samuel 17:41-47.

When David gets into the heat of the moment with Goliath, he's practically glowing with bravery. His words completely reveal where that bravery comes from. David's convinced of the power of his God and the rightness of his mission. And he says so.

It's possible to be brave and confident of victory without trusting God's power. Goliath was confident in predicting victory based on his own power. You'll hear a lot of confidence and a kind of bravery coming from some athletes, rap stars, and other successful people. They trust their own power and experience to help them win, and they brag about it.

David bragged too, but in a very different way. He said, in essence, "My God's power will defeat you; I'm only the weapon he'll use to get the job done."

If you believe that's true, then it's hard to not be brave.

7. David Didn't Hesitate—He Followed Through

Read the rest of chapter 17 to your students.

The final evidence of David's bravery came with his action. When all the thinking and talking was done, he acted. He rushed into the danger zone. He stood and fired. Then he followed through with his gruesome promise to cut off Goliath's head.

I hope your confidence in God's power to do God's work will never involve decapitating a corpse. But it *will* require action at the right time, and you'll need to see it through all the way to the finish.

Eventually it'll be time to stop debating about whether you should talk to that person, or whether you should move halfway across the country, or if you should go out for that team. When you've gathered all the information, pursued wisdom, sought good counsel, and remembered God's power in your life, it'll be time to just do it. That's what brave Christian students do.

Recap with Paul's Story

David was brave, but he was also a king and a real national hero. He was God's man in God's time. This is also God's time, and you can stand as evidence that God is real, active, and good. That might be the bravest life of all—especially when there's so much pain in our world.

The apostle Paul was an incredibly brave man. His mission from God was to keep telling people about Jesus even when they tried to kill him. He made the case that a brave Christian is one who keeps getting up again—in God's power—every time he or she gets knocked down.

Paul said that God's power in us is the only thing that can give mere human beings that kind of bravery and courage.

Read 2 Corinthians 4:7-11.

How can you live with that kind of bravery for Christ? How can you live in such a way that people see God alive in you even when you're going through the worst parts of life?

Follow David's example:

1. Get busy serving God right where you are.
2. Obey God by obeying those he's put in authority over you.
3. Ask good questions about the mission.
4. Ignore anyone who says you're too young to act bravely for God.
5. Remember and trust God's proven power in your life.
6. Don't boast about your power—boast about God's.
7. When the moment to act comes, don't hesitate. Follow through.

Conclusion Story

Wrap up the lesson by telling your class the story of Abby Sunderland, the sixteen-year-old California girl who attempted to sail solo around the world in a boat called *Wild Eyes*. You can read about her experience at abbysunderland.com.

When Abby Sunderland was attempting to sail solo around the world, her boat was damaged by a huge rogue wave that destroyed her mast. Abby had to be rescued from the middle of the ocean, and many people felt that her parents had made a mistake. Should a teenage girl do such a dangerous thing on her own? Was Abby's attempt an act of bravery or a foolish choice?

Though she wasn't on a mission from God, Abby was being brave in some ways that are similar to what we see in David's life. She served in and around boats her whole life. She had the encouragement and blessing of her parents. She had asked the questions after seeing her older brother sail around the world on his own when he was eighteen.

She ignored all those voices that said she was too young, and her testimony is that she trusted God because he had provided for her in her life. Her family is very clear about giving credit to him for the successes and safety of their children.

When the moment came, she took it and followed through. Her life is evidence that you don't have to wait to "grow up" before living your life with bravery.

Closing Prayer

Close your session in prayer by asking God to help your students grow more and more brave by learning to trust God's power and direction in their lives.

Between Sessions

Do you want to reinforce the main points of this session with your group during the week and prepare them for your next session? Here are a few things you could send out via Facebook, text, Twitter, or email.

Note: Don't send them all. It's helpful to send one the day after your group meets, and then maybe send another a couple of days later. Send teasers for the next session the day before your next meeting.

Session Reinforcement

You're not David, but you've got the same God. Be brave and sling that stone!

Be brave and obey your parents this week. God will use you if you step up for him.

Real bravery comes from trusting a really powerful God to do what he said. Are you believing him today?

Lie: You're too young to do anything hard or scary. Truth: Following Jesus is hard and scary. It matters. Be brave.

Next-Session Teasers

Got some tough decisions to make? At group this week we'll find out how to get wisdom.

Overwhelmed by everything you have to get done in your life? You need wisdom to handle it all. Find some at group this week.

Got a messy relationship or two? You need wisdom. Find some at group this week.

Got problems with your parents? You need wisdom. Find some at group this week.

Of course, these are just starter ideas. Customize these to fit your own group, group name, audience, meeting times, etc.—or just write something way better!

solomon
get wiser

How to Use the DVD

This curriculum package includes a DVD. On it, you'll find Mark presenting the main teaching points for each session. You could make use of this in one of three ways:

1. Play the DVD for your group. This could be effective if your students know Mark or if you don't have a qualified teacher available for your group. It could also be helpful to use the DVD if your group chooses to break up into smaller groups during the teaching time. Another idea would be to watch the video together and then go back through the main points of the teaching more conversationally, using the leader's guide for reference. (Note: The DVD doesn't cover the discussion questions, activities, or other interactive material in this leader's guide.)

2. Use Mark's teaching as part of your preparation. Notice what he emphasizes and how he delivers the content.

3. Skip it! You don't need the DVD to make full use of the curriculum. It's included as a possible enhancement for those who wish to use it.

Introduction

Developmentally, the students we're working with tend to have very black-and-white thinking. Christian students, especially, can be very concerned with what's right and what's wrong—even when they fully intend to do something wrong! We've all done it, carefully structuring questions about morality to figure out exactly how far we could go before we were "wrong."

And, of course, God *does* provide moral absolutes. We need to help teens understand the difference between right and wrong and see why it matters to God. It's a dangerous thing to skip the black-and-white thinking phase.

But this session is less about right and wrong and more about better and best. We want our students to set a standard for themselves higher than just not doing wrong things. If all they accomplish is coming to church at the right times and not sampling sex, alcohol, or drugs, then what mediocre Christians—and humans—they'll be.

The world may not expect kids to have the skill of choosing the better of two pretty good things, but *we* can expect that of them. God does. And we'd love for them to begin to expect that of themselves.

Let's raise that bar a notch today.

What's the Story?

It's easier to discover meaningful truth in the context of a good story.

The main story for this session takes place when David's son Solomon is the new king of Israel. He's far from perfect when it comes to choosing to do right rather than wrong. His motives are messy, and his obedience looks sloppy. But in a key moment, he recognizes his greatest need and asks God to give it to him.

We can all relate, and hopefully our students will see parallels in their own lives with that of a newbie king of Israel.

We'll also tell some supporting stories to help round out our need for God's wisdom, including a story from Ecclesiastes about a wise man who saves a city. In addition, we'll hear the story of a seventeen-year-old Californian named Steven Ortiz who used some large helpings of practical wisdom to trade his way from an old cell phone to a Porsche Boxster.

What's the Point?

We hope to accomplish two big things with this Bible study session:

1. To increase our students' appetite and sense of need for God's wisdom

2. To help our students understand how they can find and use God's wisdom in their lives right now

What You'll Need

Whiteboard, chalkboard, overhead projector, or large sheet of paper to write on

Bibles

Activity/Group Discussion
Who Needs More Wisdom?

For this activity/discussion you'll need a chalkboard, whiteboard, overhead projector, or large sheet of paper to write on.

This activity will include quite a bit of group discussion as you and your students talk about what kinds of people need more wisdom to be successful in their lives and jobs.

Before you start, your students need a good working definition of *wisdom*. For now, you can define it for your students in two ways. (We'll expand on this definition during the Bible study.) Wisdom is (a) skill at using information to make good decisions and (b) making the best choice from several pretty good options. Write these definitions down for your students to see.

Explain that you're going to look at several types of people and make a list of who needs the most wisdom. Start by writing down these two life roles: PARENT and TEACHER. Ask for opinions about who needs more wisdom and why.

As the conversation unfolds, remind your students that we're not talking about how much a person knows, but rather what choices they make with that information. For this particular debate, you could say that a teacher needs wisdom to make choices that will influence a lot more kids. But you could also say the influence of a parent makes a much bigger impact than any one teacher in a person's life.

After a few minutes, ask everyone to vote by a show of hands and then list the two roles in that order. Next, introduce the role of DOCTOR and ask your students if a doctor would need more or less wisdom than the teacher or the parent. Allow input for just a minute or two and then vote, re-creating your list in order.

Next, ask about the role of an AIR TRAFFIC CONTROLLER. Again, allow a little input and then vote. Then do the same with HEAD OF A MAJOR CORPORATION and then again with PRESIDENT OF THE UNITED STATES.

Of course, feel free to add your own roles or positions to this list. It should be interesting to see which roles your group of teens thinks would require the most wisdom. Once you have a list of all the roles in order of who your group thinks needs more wisdom, introduce one last role: TEENAGER. (Or STUDENT or whatever word you think best characterizes the people in your group.)

Give your students a little room to discuss whether they see their role as needing more or less wisdom than the others on the list. Then steer the conversation by making the following suggestion:

Maybe a teenager in all the different roles he or she has to play needs more wisdom than anyone. How can someone hope to be wise as a parent, teacher, doctor, business leader, or even the President if that person doesn't start to gain wisdom as a teenager?

Allow for a final vote, but emphasize the point that being successful in all of the different roles they have in life right now requires lots of wisdom. It's not enough that they just make the right choices—they also need to make hard choices between pretty good options.

Show empathy by expressing that at their stage of life, it's often really hard to know the best thing to do in a relationship, in balancing time between lots of different responsibilities, in deciding what extracurricular activities are worth doing, in relating with people in authority (especially the foolish ones), and in following Jesus. Who faces more pressure in his or her daily life than a teenager who truly wants to honor God, do well in sports or school, be a good friend, earn money, and get along with parents?

As you head into the Bible study, make this final point:

Wisdom matters for everyone—and everyone can get wisdom, including every person in this room right now.

Bible Study

Backstory

Introduce the Bible study by giving a brief backstory to show how Solomon became the king of Israel at such a young age. Explain the following in your own words:

Last week, we talked about how David bravely battled the giant Goliath when David was probably still a teenager. He was able to be brave because he was absolutely convinced that God was powerful and God was with him. David went on from that moment to become the greatest king in Israel's history.

Two weeks ago, we talked about resisting temptation. We ended that session with a story about how King David gave in to temptation. He had sex with another man's wife, Bathsheba, and then murdered that man to cover up his sin when Bathsheba became pregnant.

That baby died; God forgave David. Then David and Bathsheba married, and one of their other sons was Solomon. When David died, Solomon became the king of Israel at the young age of twenty. He was a remarkable person, but he was far from perfect—as we're about to see in today's Bible study.

Scripture: 1 Kings 3

The Big Question: What can we learn from Solomon's story about getting wiser?

1. Solomon Disobeyed God Sometimes

Ask a student to read 1 Kings 3:1-3 out loud to the group. Emphasize the following in your own words:

As the new king of Israel, Solomon appears to have understood that he had huge shoes to fill. His dad, David, was a great king. Solomon knew that part of his father's greatness had to do with David's obedience to and relationship with God. Solomon wanted that, too.

So Solomon obeyed God . . . mostly. Right away, we're told that he married an Egyptian princess to make peace with

Egypt—even though God's Law said not to marry non-Israelites. Solomon did a wrong thing to try to make a good thing happen. Later in Solomon's life, it became clear how foolish that was.

The other thing we're told is that Solomon also broke God's Law by offering sacrifices in the high places. God told Israel to offer sacrifices at the tabernacle where the ark of the covenant was. But Israel had picked up a habit from other nations of offering sacrifices in other places. Partly, it was more convenient. Partly, it was just a popular thing to do.

Solomon, the king, did it, too. He didn't take that command seriously.

Maybe we can relate to Solomon in this way. We might want to be close to God, but we don't take some of his commands to us very seriously, either. We can be kind of casual about what God tells us to do.

Is that okay? Nope. Solomon suffered some painful consequences because of his sinful choices. Here's the thing, though: Solomon's sins did not keep God from giving him wisdom. God showed Solomon grace and helped him to be wise.

Don't believe that God won't help you to be wise because you've sinned too much or because you still want to sin. Through Jesus, God gives grace to us as his children. You may still pay heavy consequences for sinful choices, but God will give you wisdom—and that'll help you to make better choices as you continue to learn to trust him.

2. Solomon Loved God and Showed It

Ask another student to read 1 Kings 3:4 out loud.

Solomon loved the Lord, and his life showed it. He mostly obeyed God. And he didn't obey just to keep God from being mad at him. He did it because he loved and trusted God as a Father.

That's also why he offered a thousand burnt offerings at this place called Gibeon. God's Law required Israelites to participate in offering animals as sacrifice, but the Law didn't require a thousand of them at once. Solomon wanted to show in a big way that he loved God and was putting all of his hope and trust in God.

How does your life show that you love God? Do you show it by obeying what the Bible teaches? Do you show it by doing more than the minimum you think God requires of you?

Evidence that we love God might show up in how often we talk to him or the kinds of things we say when we pray. You could also say that how and how often we read God's truth for us in the Bible is evidence of whether we love him or not.

3. God Responded to Solomon's Heart

Ask a third student to read out loud to the group, this time from 1 Kings 3:5.

On one hand, Solomon was casually disobeying God's Law by offering sacrifices how and where he did. On the other hand, Solomon truly loved God and tried to show it.

The word *grace* means getting a good thing you didn't earn. The word *mercy* is a little different: Mercy is *not* getting a bad thing you *did* earn. God showed Solomon grace and mercy in this moment; he chose to respond to Solomon's heart and not to his disobedience.

Has God shown grace and mercy to you? How? (Encourage an answer or two to these questions. The big idea is that God has given us both grace and mercy by forgiving our sins through faith in Jesus and giving us credit for Jesus' sinless life.)

God also responds to our hearts. Listen to this verse from the book of James in the New Testament: "Come near to God and he will come near to you" (James 4:8).

God is amazingly generous. Every time one of God's children moves closer to him, he moves closer to him or her. He loves that we come to him on our own because we love and trust him. His heart responds to our hearts.

In this moment with Solomon, God responded with maybe the greatest offer ever: "Ask for whatever you want me to give you."

What would you ask for? It gets our wheels spinning, doesn't it? Money. Fame. Relationships. Sex. Power. Greatness. Anything you can think up, God is promising to give. You probably already know what Solomon asked for—let's look at why he asked for it.

4. Solomon Understood That He Needed Wisdom

Have someone else read 1 Kings 3:6-9 to the group.

Solomon showed that he understood three major things here. First, his job mattered. The work God had given him to do in the world mattered right now. Second, he didn't know the best way to do that job. On his own, he'd never do it as well as it needed to be done. Third, he needed God's help to figure it out.

Some of you don't believe that what God's given you to do in the world right now matters. You think it's not important what kind of child you are to your parents or what kind of student or athlete or employee you are. You think it doesn't matter how you begin to use your spiritual gifts to serve other people at church.

If that's what you think, you're wrong. If the God of the universe puts you in a position or gives you a job to do—and he has—*it matters*. It's important to him, so it's important. Solomon understood that.

Second, some of you don't think you need wisdom to do the jobs God has given you. You think you're wise enough to be "just" a child to your parents, or a student, or an athlete, or a babysitter, or a VBS helper, or whatever it is you'll do this year. And maybe you can get through those things without God's wisdom. But to do anything the best way it can be done, you need to admit that you don't yet know everything there is to know about it. We all need to admit that we're not perfect—that there's always room to do the work God's given us better. That's called humility.

The book of James quotes something Solomon wrote in Proverbs 3:34:

God opposes the proud but shows favor to the humble. (James 4:6)

Third, some of us know we need help, but we don't think God's the one who can give it to us. We think our help will come from a person, from the Internet, or from a training program. And maybe God will use one of those things to help us, but Solomon knew that God is the ultimate source of help.

Do we know that?

5. God Gives Wisdom

Another reader can take the group through 1 Kings 3:10-14.

God liked Solomon's answer to his offer. He liked it so much that he not only promised to make Solomon the wisest man who ever was or would be—he also promised that if Solomon would keep obeying him, then God would make him rich and honored in the world and would give him a long life.

Wisdom can be gained in a few ways. You can learn it through experience—usually the hard way by making a foolish choice and saying, "I'll never do that again!" You can learn wisdom through study, especially of the wise sayings in wisdom books in the Bible.

But you can also get wisdom directly from God as a gift. That's what happened to Solomon. And that's what can happen for you. God gives wisdom.

Let's listen to James again:

> If any of you lacks wisdom, you should ask God, who gives generously to all without finding fault, and it will be given to you. (James 1:5)

That's a promise from God to his children that he'll give us wisdom when we ask for it to help us make the best decisions we can. If you understand that you need wisdom to do what God's given you to do, you can ask him for it. He'll give it to you—even if you still don't obey him perfectly all of the time.

However, there's a condition to that promise:

> But when you ask, you must believe and not doubt, because the one who doubts is like a wave of the sea, blown and tossed by the wind. That person should not expect to receive anything from the Lord. Such a person is double-minded and unstable in all they do. (James 1:6-8)

In other words, God gives wisdom to people who ask and believe that God gives wisdom to people who ask.

He doesn't want us to ask him for wisdom because "it's worth a shot." Or "Who knows? That might work!" He doesn't want us to ask for wisdom from him, Mohammed, Buddha, and an idol, hoping that one of them might give it to us.

He wants us to see him as our only source of real wisdom—the kind of wisdom that gives us everything we need to make the best choices in the work he gives us to do.

6. Solomon Immediately Acted Wisely by Obeying God
Have someone read 1 Kings 3:15.

With the wisdom God had just given him, Solomon seems to have finally understood how foolish he was to offer sacrifices at the high places.

The first wise thing he did was to obey God's Law. He went straight to Jerusalem and sacrificed offerings there—rather than offering more sacrifices at Gibeon.

It's always wise to obey God. Always. Disobeying God is always a foolish choice. Always. Solomon wouldn't always act wisely in that way, but he understood it on this day.

If you ever face a tough decision and one of the options you're considering involves disobeying something the Bible tells you to do, you can be sure that's a foolish choice. Every time.

Recap with a Story from Ecclesiastes
It's believed that Solomon also wrote the book of Ecclesiastes in the Bible. In that book, he tells a very short story about wisdom.

Read Ecclesiastes 9:13-16 out loud to your students.

This is a war story. An underdog story. An unlikely hero story. We don't know if Solomon was thinking of something that really happened or if this was a popular tale of his day, but he wrote that he was impressed by the poor man's wisdom.

How did the man use wisdom to save his city from the powerful king? We don't know. But we do know where the solution came from: wisdom.

Notice something, though: Solomon points out that the man used wisdom to save the city, but that wisdom didn't make him rich or popular. God provides wisdom (or helps us to find it) to come up with the answer to the big and little questions of life. But wisdom is not about fame and fortune; it's about living a life that makes sense from God's perspective.

If you're not facing a major decision today, you'll face one before long. And you'll face a hundred minor decisions between now and then. How will you choose? Which way will you go?

Solomon gave this advice to his kids about how to make all those choices:

> Listen, my sons, to a father's instruction;
>> pay attention and gain understanding.
> I give you sound learning,
>> so do not forsake my teaching.
> For I too was a son to my father,
>> still tender, and cherished by my mother.
> Then he taught me, and he said to me,
>> "Take hold of my words with all your heart;
>> keep my commands, and you will live.
> Get wisdom, get understanding;
>> do not forget my words or turn away from them.
> Do not forsake wisdom, and she will protect you;
>> love her, and she will watch over you.
> The beginning of wisdom is this: Get wisdom.
>> Though it cost all you have, get understanding.
> Cherish her, and she will exalt you;
>> embrace her, and she will honor you. (Proverbs 4:1-8)

Solomon sat his kids down with the most important advice he could give to them. It wasn't about how to be rich or how to be famous. He wanted them to do one thing: "Get wisdom!"

Even if it made them poor and unpopular, Solomon wanted his kids to "get wisdom!"

And where did his wisdom come from?

1. It didn't come from being perfect and never sinning.
2. He loved God and showed it.
3. God responded to Solomon's heart with grace and mercy.
4. Solomon knew he needed wisdom and asked for it.

5. God gives wisdom.

6. Solomon acted wisely by obeying God.

Do you need wisdom? Yes, you do. How will you get wisdom from God?

Conclusion Story

Wrap up the lesson by telling your class the story of Steven Ortiz of Glendora, California:[1]

Steven Ortiz used Craigslist to trade and barter his way from an old cell phone to a Porsche Boxster. Yes, we're talking about an actual, functioning, great-looking, convertible sports car.

How'd he do it? You could call it practical wisdom. Steven became wise in the art of "trading up," swapping less valuable things for more valuable things. It was hard work, and it took him two years. But he did it.

Along the way, he owned an iPod, a MacBook Pro laptop, dirt bikes, and other cars and trucks.

He told one reporter, "A lot of my friends come up to me and tell me, 'You want to trade my phone for a car? Try to get me a Ferrari.' I tell them it's not that easy. It takes time and patience, definitely."

The story said that Steven knew a little bit about electronics and cars and how to use sites like Craigslist. But the wisdom came in what Steven did with that knowledge. He put what he knew to good use in what became a kind of business.

Does it matter that he did it all as a teenager? Nope. Wisdom is available to everybody. If Steven was able to do that with trading on the Internet, what could you do with your life for God using the wisdom he will give to you?

Don't wait until you grow up to find out.

Closing Prayer

Close your session in prayer by thanking God that he gives wisdom to his children when they ask him for it and trust that he'll provide.

Also thank him that he provides wisdom in the Bible and through wise people in our lives. Ask him to help every single person in the room with you to admit the need for God's wisdom, to trust him for it, and to use God's wisdom to best do whatever he gives each of you to do.

Between Sessions

Do you want to reinforce the main points of this session with your group during the week and prepare them for your next session? Here are a few things you could send out via Facebook, text, Twitter, or email.

Note: Don't send them all. It's helpful to send one the day after your group meets, and then maybe send another a couple of days later. Send teasers for the next session the day before your next meeting.

Session Reinforcement

God gives wisdom to people who believe he will. Have you asked him for some?

What do you need wisdom for this week? Where will you find it?

Pride = NOT asking God for wisdom and NOT looking for it in the Bible.

"Get wisdom. Though it cost all you have, get understanding." Don't wait for later!

Next-Session Teasers

Does it matter if you do what everyone else is doing? Why? Come to group this week and find out.

Sin is easy. Saying no is hard. Get stronger. Find out how at group this week.

Don't ask questions. Just eat, drink, watch, play, think what everyone does. Or stand strong. Your choice. Find out more at group this week.

What do you do when God's way and your friends' ways go in different directions? Come talk about it at group this week.

Of course, these are just starter ideas. Customize these to fit your own group, group name, audience, meeting times, etc.—or just write something way better!

daniel and friends
stand stronger

How to Use the DVD

This curriculum package includes a DVD. On it, you'll find Mark presenting the main teaching points for each session. You could make use of this in one of three ways:

1. Play the DVD for your group. This could be effective if your students know Mark or if you don't have a qualified teacher available for your group. It could also be helpful to use the DVD if your group chooses to break up into smaller groups during the teaching time. Another idea would be to watch the video together and then go back through the main points of the teaching more conversationally, using the leader's guide for reference. (Note: The DVD doesn't cover the discussion questions, activities, or other interactive material in this leader's guide.)

2. Use Mark's teaching as part of your preparation. Notice what he emphasizes and how he delivers the content.

3. Skip it! You don't need the DVD to make full use of the curriculum. It's included as a possible enhancement for those who wish to use it.

Introduction

The message to teenagers to stand up to peer pressure and do the right thing is as old as youth ministry itself. At times in recent church history, it has felt like the only message we had for students was *Don't*!

Number one on the "don't list" is, of course, sex. In some corners, purity was the drum we banged loudest and most frequently. We'd quickly follow that with the after-school special PSA of, *Don't drink. Don't do drugs. Stay in school.*

Yes, those messages to teens *are* important. And biblical. And relevant to the culture. The problem is that when we emphasize the don'ts to the exclusion of the rest of God's Word, we also deliver the not-so-subtle message that *God doesn't really expect you to do anything meaningful in your life for him right now—just avoid doing anything too destructive.*

There's no less compelling prize to compete for than the one for nonparticipation.

That's not our message this week. We're less interested in telling our teenagers to stand stronger for God *against* their culture than we are in telling them to stand stronger for God *in* their culture. We want them to hear the call to help his reputation grow by attempting excellence in every secular arena he puts them in.

Yes, just saying no is part of that equation. But so is saying, "Yes," "Why?" "How?" "Count me in," and "Why not now?"

What's the Story?

It's easier to discover meaningful truth in the context of a good story.

Your students may be less familiar with the story that's told in Daniel 1 than with some of the other stories you've told in this study, but it's a great one! In addition to its ancient and exotic setting and its focus on some (possibly) teenage captives, the story also offers strong parallels to the world your students live in right now—and the extraordinary things they might accomplish with big and practical trust in God.

Daniel and his three friends were conquered, captured, and enslaved by a king who planned to strategically enculturate them so as to weaken their dependence on and obedience to God and lure them into dependence on and obedience to the king and his gods. With impressive results, Daniel and the others refused to violate their convictions about obeying God, while fully welcoming the opportunity to thrive in every other aspect of this new culture.

To support this story, we'll reference a story from later in Daniel and his friends' lives when they were willing to die for the sake of obeying God—only to see God protect them and make himself more famous than ever before in that foreign culture.

Finally, we'll take a quick look at the story of Chick-fil-A owner Truett Cathy's decision to keep his restaurants closed on Sundays because of his deeply held Christian convictions—and the surprising result.

What's the Point?

We hope to accomplish one big thing with this Bible study session:

1. To inspire our students to stand stronger for their convictions about biblical truth while participating with enthusiasm and excellence in their culture

What You'll Need

Bibles

A way to display student-made or other videos to your group (optional—see the Activity at the end of the Bible study)

Bible Study

Backstory

Introduce the Bible study by giving a brief backstory of the history that brought Daniel and his friends to be captives in Babylon as teenagers (or "young men"). Explain the following in your own words:

Daniel and his three friends, Hananiah, Mishael, and Azariah grew up during a terrible time in Israel's history. God repeatedly warned that he would allow Israel to be conquered by her enemies if the people didn't obey the law he'd given to Moses.

Of the twelve tribes, the northern ten, known as Israel, had been conquered and dispersed more than a hundred years before Daniel came along. His nation, Judah, was made up of the remaining two tribes. The people of Judah obeyed God

sometimes, but mostly they didn't. So God eventually sent his judgment.

That judgment came in the form of the most powerful nation on earth at the time. Nebuchadnezzar, king of Babylon, conquered Jerusalem, the capital of Judah. Today's story starts with that event.

Notice something, though: God judged Judah for her long history of unfaithfulness to him. But Daniel and his friends were the exception. They were so loyal to God and his law that they were wiling to risk their lives to follow it, even as captives in Babylon.

Scripture: Daniel 1

The Big Question: What can we learn from the story of Daniel and his friends about standing stronger?

1. Daniel and Friends Knew They Were Foreigners

Ask a student to read Daniel 1:1-4 out loud to the group. Emphasize the following in your own words:

Aside from being captives of war far from home, Daniel and his friends had a lot going for them. Because they were royalty and strong, good-looking guys, they'd been placed in an elite training program created by the king of Babylon.

They would not be mistreated, *and* they were going to receive the best of everything—including what may have been the best possible education available anywhere in the world at that time. It would be a little like being recruited to go to an Ivy League school—if you were forced to do it after your hometown had been defeated in a war.

Daniel and his friends likely were used to being treated well, but this would have been a whole new and very impressive world full of fascinating, sophisticated, and wealthy people from many different places.

It would have been easy for Daniel and his friends to forget where they came from. It would have been easy for them to say,

"Our home is gone. This is our home now. We're going to try to blend in and make the best of it."

But we'll see as we get further into this story that Daniel, Hananiah, Mishael, and Azariah always understood that their home was in Jerusalem. They were Israelites. They were foreigners. They would never fully belong here, even as they eventually became more and more successful and respected.

As Christians, we're also told to remember that this isn't our home. Listen to 1 Peter 1:17: "Since you call on a Father who judges each person's work impartially, live out your time as foreigners here in reverent fear."

The Bible describes us as citizens of heaven, soon to be headed home after our lives here are finished. We're not locals. We're not from around here. That means we must find a way to live by the standards of our own country while living in a foreign land—just like Daniel and the boys.

2. Daniel and Friends Experienced Intense Pressure to Conform and Forget God

Ask another student to read Daniel 1:5-7 out loud.

Apparently, part of King Nebuchadnezzar's strategy for controlling the nations he conquered was to take the best of the best from each conquered people, strip them of their own religions and identities, turn them into high-achieving Babylonians—and then maybe send them back to their homes one day to rule their nations for him. Or maybe he just wanted to be served by the best people the world had to offer.

Either way, the king started by feeding each new recruit into the system by giving him Babylon's best wine, food, and education—after giving him a new, Babylonian name to make it clear his gods were dead and he was under new religious management.

Here are the meanings for the names Daniel and his friends came in with alongside the meanings of the new names they were given:

Daniel ("God has judged" or "God is my judge") became Belteshazzar ("Lady [wife of the god Bel], protect the king").

Hananiah ("Yahweh is gracious") became Shadrach ("I am fearful [of a god]" or "command of Aku [the moon god]").

Mishael ("Who is what God is?") became Meshach ("I am of little account [before my god]" or "Who is like Aku?").

Azariah ("Yahweh is a helper") became Abednego ("servant of Nebo [another god]").

Next, they were assigned to eat the very same food the king ate, and it wasn't considered optional. The Babylonians believed that their food and strong wine helped to make their minds and bodies strong.

Daniel and his friends had two problems. First, they could not truly own the new names they were given. They would answer to them when they had to, but among themselves they would retain the God-honoring names their parents had given them and not accept the idol-worshiping names assigned to them.

Second, they were convinced that God's law wouldn't allow them to eat the meat or drink the wine that they were being given. It may have been that the wine was especially strong, or that the wine and meat had been offered to these false idols, or simply that the food would have been ceremonially unclean. Whatever the reason, their understanding was that to eat this food would be to dishonor and disobey their God, the God of Israel.

But what could they do?

If you haven't already, you'll someday also face intense pressure to conform. The world has a plan for you, an expectation for what you'll participate in and what you won't. Romans 12 calls it a "pattern" into which everyone is expected to fit.

Listen to what it says:

Do not conform to the pattern of this world, but be transformed by the renewing of your mind. Then you will be able to test and approve what God's will is—his good, pleasing and perfect will. (Romans 12:2)

Let's find out how Daniel and his friends chose to live out what they believed.

3. Daniel and Friends Resolved Not to Violate Their Convictions

Ask a third student to read out loud to the group, this time from Daniel 1:8.

They were foreigners in a strange land. Treated as princes, but under extreme pressure to give up their own names and faith in God, Daniel chose how he would respond to it all: "But Daniel resolved not to . . ."

Standing strong for your convictions when the pressure is on to go with the crowd starts with one thing: a choice—a rebellion against the culture that expects you to change. A statement: "I will not."

Did you notice that Daniel apparently had to start out making that decision on his own? His friends join him in a verse or two, but Daniel seemed to make the resolution first.

Too often, we simply try to skip this step. We know the right thing to do, but we hold off on resolving until the very last moment, kind of waiting to see which way we'll go. With that strategy, we almost always go whichever way is easiest, not necessarily the way that's best.

Daniel made a choice and then took action. Don't wait and just hope you'll do the right thing when the time comes.

4. Daniel and Friends Came Up with Creative Alternatives

Have someone else read Daniel 1:9-16 to the group.

First, Daniel resolved not to eat the king's food or drink his wine. He made the choice to do the thing he knew would honor God. And then he acted, and God responded.

Daniel went to those placed in authority over him and respectfully asked to be allowed not to eat or drink anything but veggies and water. God gave the guy a soft spot for Daniel and his friends, so he told them why that wouldn't work: "You'll be too weak."

Here's the creative alternative part: Daniel said, "Test us. See how we do. Why not try it?" When you're appealing to someone in authority, offering a creative alternative to their decision almost never hurts—and it often opens a door to surprising results.

Daniel showed that he understood what the official was concerned about, and then he addressed his concern with a new approach.

There's another way to stand for our convictions. We can become angry, unreasonable, and judgmental. We can criticize everyone who has anything to do with the wrong choice we're being asked to participate in. In short, we can be a real jerk about it.

You might know some Christians who've stood up for what was right in the most wrong and hurtful way possible. That's not what Daniel does here. He won't give in no matter what, but he also won't be unkind, disrespectful, or unreasonable.

Instead, he relies on God to provide and starts by thinking of a mutually beneficial way around the wrong thing he's being asked to do.

You can do this, too. Whether the choice you're being asked to make is coming from friends or someone in authority, you can always say no with kindness—and you can often say no with creativity.

5. Daniel and Friends Said Yes to What They Could and Fully Participated

Another reader can take the group through Daniel 1:17.

After taking their stand on the issue of honoring God in the food they ate, Daniel and his friends appear to have jumped into their training with everything they had. They used the abilities God blessed them with to fully understand what they were being taught—to the point that they became the best students around.

Christians can miss this response in two ways. On the one hand, we can be so afraid of looking foolish or being rejected by people in our culture that we're not strong enough to say no to things that we know God doesn't want us to do. That weakness comes from not trusting God.

On the other hand, sometimes we're strong enough to say no to compromising our convictions, but we're not strong enough to stay in the culture—and in relationship with other people in the culture—and say yes to all of the things available in which to participate. That weakness also comes from not trusting God to help us use the talents and gifts he's given us to live for him right in the middle of the culture he's put us in.

God wants both from you. He wants you to honor him by saying no to participating in sinful things in the culture. And he wants you to honor him by being honorable while participating in all of the things you're good at in the culture.

With God's help, you're strong enough to do both of these, just as Daniel and his friends did.

6. Daniel and Friends Earned the Respect of the Culture

Have someone read Daniel 1:18-20.

Daniel and his friends didn't just survive the ungodly influences of their culture by holding on to their faith and refusing to do wrong—they thrived right in the middle of the culture. They became the most impressive graduates of the king's training program and earned the respect of all the unbelievers around them.

In other words, God made himself more famous because these guys were willing to say yes to their heathen culture wherever they could. God even gave them the skills to be the best of the bunch.

Talented Christians today often rise to the top of their secular fields of sports, science, arts, philosophy, or business. They get involved. They participate. They try hard. They don't refuse to spend time with anyone who doesn't believe in Jesus. They just refuse to participate in sinful actions, and then they show up for everything else and do their absolute best.

Peter wrote a letter to Christians who were living in a world that didn't like them much. He told them to remember that they had a home in heaven and not to get involved in sinful choices as if they'll always live here. But he also told them to be in relationships with unbelievers so God could be glorified.

Listen to this:

Dear friends, I urge you, as foreigners and exiles, to abstain from sinful desires, which wage war against your soul. Live such good lives among the pagans that, though they accuse you of doing wrong, they may see your good deeds and glorify God on the day he visits us. (1 Peter 2:11-12)

Maybe you need to say no to some more things you feel pressured to participate in. Or maybe you need to say yes to some more things. Let's talk about how that looks in our own world for a few minutes.

Activity

Five Questions

Probably the best way to help your students to learn to practice this Christian ideal of standing strong against the world's sinful expectations—while standing strong in the middle of the culture by participating in it—is to show them some examples.

We've thought of a few ways you could do that at this point in the session:

1. Video Interviews

A week ahead of time, select one or a few of your students and ask them to interview and videotape a few Christian students they know who've had to stand up and say no to pressure to go along with sinful choices, but who've also said yes to getting involved in secular activities.

Your students could take theses videos with a phone or any other kind of camera. Just make sure you've got a way to display the video to the group (for example, on a computer monitor after they email it to you).

You could provide your interviewers with these five questions to make their job as easy as possible:

1. Talk about a time when you had to say no to pressure to compromise your Christian convictions.
2. How did you handle it and what was the result?
3. Would you do anything differently now?
4. What are some things you do that give you a chance to interact with lots of unbelievers?
5. How does being involved in that help you to represent Christ even when you're not talking about him?

Note: Make sure you preview the videos first and select the best ones before showing them to your group.

2. College Students
You might consider contacting a few strong Christian college students during the week before this session. Ask them the same five questions. If you can do it on video, great! If not, you could have them respond by email, in an IM exchange, or even by having them show up in person.

3. Student Testimonies
Another approach might be to select a few students a week ahead of time—students you know who've stood strong in their culture—and ask them to come prepared to answer those five questions themselves.

Group Discussion
Live Well in Your World
Close this part of your study by having some frank group discussion about some of the issues covered in this session. A few of the questions below might help:

Can you relate to Daniel and his friends at all? Do you ever feel pressure to participate in things you know are wrong?

What do you think are some of the best ways to handle those situations?

In what kinds of ways are you or your friends most often expected to participate in sinful choices?

Can two different Christians have different feelings about whether something is wrong to participate in or not? Why is that?

How much easier is it to stand for something you believe is right when you have two or three friends taking the same stand with you?

Can you think of any examples of coming up with a creative alternative to avoid (in a kind or respectful way) participating in something you felt was wrong?

What are some of the ways you're participating with unbelievers in your culture right now?

Do you or others you know ever hesitate to participate in things because most of the people involved won't be Christians?

Have you ever seen someone be strong in standing for his or her convictions but weak in getting fully involved in participating in something because of fear of relationships with unbelievers? What's wrong with that?

Have you seen any strong Christians in your world or in other places earn the respect of unbelievers because they showed up, worked hard, and did a great job? Do you think that's helpful to the reputation of Christ?

Recap with the Lives of Daniel's Friends

During their first three years in Babylon, Daniel and his friends stood strong for God, and God helped them to succeed in a big way. They became respected and influential men in the kingdom.

Sometimes, though, standing strong for your convictions doesn't exactly work out that way. Sometimes it can cost everything you have. Right now, people around the world are paying with their lives for putting their trust in Jesus and refusing to continue to participate in religions they believe are false.

Daniel and his friends were eventually ordered to their deaths for their refusal to participate in worshiping false gods—but God saved them, even then.

In Daniel 3, we read about how King Nebuchadnezzar made a law that everyone should bow down and worship a huge golden statue whenever a musical cue was sounded in Babylon. Daniel's friends Shadrach, Meshach, and Abednego stood strong and refused to participate. They were miraculously saved from burning up when they were thrown into a super-hot furnace.

Before that moment of glory, though, they faced a moment of decision. They had already resolved in their hearts not to bow to the idol. This is how they explained it to the furious king:

> "King Nebuchadnezzar, we do not need to defend ourselves before you in this matter. If we are thrown into the blazing furnace, the God we serve is able to deliver us from it, and he will deliver us from Your Majesty's hand. But even if he does not, we want you to know, Your Majesty, that we will not serve your gods or worship the image of gold you have set up." (Daniel 3:16-18)

In order to stand stronger in our culture, we as Christians must resolve in our hearts to say no to the pressure to sin and yes to the opportunity to participate with all we have in whatever we can do for God's glory.

And we have to be willing to pay whatever it costs—even if that means not getting what we hope for in the moment.

Conclusion Story

Wrap up the lesson by telling your group the following story of S. Truett Cathy, the founder and owner of the Chick-fil-A chain of restaurants:

When S. Truett Cathy launched the Chick-fil-A chain, he felt convicted that it wouldn't be honoring to God or the people who worked for him to have the restaurants open on Sundays.

As far as we know, he didn't insist that it was wrong for others to be open on Sundays. He didn't ask for the world to be changed. In fact, many Christians didn't necessarily agree with his position. But he stuck by what he believed was right and God-honoring.

He was told over and over again that he couldn't do that. It's not how business works. It's not done. You'll fail. You'll never make it.

Of course, it's a story with a happy ending. The Chick-fil-A chain has been, and continues to be, phenomenally successful. Mr. Cathy attempts to give all of the glory for his success to God. And the stores are still closed on Sundays.

The point of Mr. Cathy's story isn't that every Christian business owner must close on Sundays. It's that God honors our choices to stand stronger for our convictions about how he wants us to live in our culture.

Closing Prayer

Close your session in prayer by thanking God for all the stories you've talked about of people who stood stronger for him while fully participating in the culture he placed them in. Ask him to help you and your students stand strong for what you're convinced God would want you to do this week. Ask him to be honored in your lives.

Between Sessions

Do you want to reinforce the main points of this session with your group during the week and prepare them for your next session? Here are a few things you could send out via Facebook, text, Twitter, or email.

Note: Don't send them all. It's helpful to send one the day after your group meets, and then maybe send another a couple of days later. Send teasers for the next session the day before your next meeting.

Session Reinforcement

Are you standing stronger this week? What are you saying no and yes to?

What will it cost you to stand strong against the pattern of the world this week?

Give it all you've got this week. Say yes to doing your best for God.

Having a tough time saying no to sin? Get a strong friend to say no with you.

Next-Session Teasers

Are you on a mission from God? If yes, what is it? If not, why not? Come to group and find out.

What has God called you to do this week? That's what group is all about. Join us!

God wants you to do hard things. Right now. Things that will matter forever. What are you waiting for?

Why did God give a teenage girl one of the hardest jobs in history? Because that's what he does! What hard thing does he want you to do?

Of course, these are just starter ideas. Customize these to fit your own group, group name, audience, meeting times, etc.—or just write something way better!

mary
accept the mission now

How to Use the DVD

This curriculum package includes a DVD. On it, you'll find Mark presenting the main teaching points for each session. You could make use of this in one of three ways:

1. Play the DVD for your group. This could be effective if your students know Mark or if you don't have a qualified teacher available for your group. It could also be helpful to use the DVD if your group chooses to break up into smaller groups during the teaching time. Another idea would be to watch the video together and then go back through the main points of the teaching more conversationally, using the leader's guide for reference. (Note: The DVD doesn't cover the discussion questions, activities, or other interactive material in this leader's guide.)

2. Use Mark's teaching as part of your preparation. Notice what he emphasizes and how he delivers the content.

3. Skip it! You don't need the DVD to make full use of the curriculum. It's included as a possible enhancement for those who wish to use it.

Introduction

In our sixth and final session, we're hoping to help our students really make the connection that God has a mission for them *right now*. God uses believers, Christians, followers of Jesus regardless of age, income, GPA, or popularity. We want to help our teens see that there are no missing pieces to wait for. Today they can start doing hard things, meaningful things, and essential things for God wherever he's put them.

We must be aware that in saying this to our students, we'll be speaking against some of the messages of their culture. That may include messages they've caught from friends, the media, and even their parents.

Our societal practice of extended adolescence through the teen years and then into college and beyond is a relatively recent change, historically speaking. One result is that students can be left with the impression that they're always preparing for a "real life" that may not arrive until they're in their late twenties.

The inevitable result for anyone who sees his or her life as practice or preparation for something significant later on is that it's easy not to take responsibility for his or her choices: *Nothing really matters until my "real" life finally starts. I'll get serious then.*

We want our students to hear from God's Word that they're in the middle of their real life *right now*, that God has plans for them today that have eternal consequences, and that it matters that they accept the mission and carry it out.

What's the Story?

It's easier to discover meaningful truth in the context of a good story. And there's a downside to thinking of Mary's story as only a Christmas story: It feels hopelessly familiar and too connected to the emotions and pressures of the season. During Christmas we also tend to play up the sentimentality and package the tale for children.

Hopefully, you won't be teaching this lesson too close to December. But even if you are, you have the opportunity to tell this story of a (probably) teenage girl who was confronted with a specific mission from God to do a weird, wonderful, and really hard thing.

Why did she accept the mission? How did she accept it? And what did God get out of using her to accomplish it? That's what the story will show us.

What's the Point?

We hope to accomplish two big things with this Bible study session:

1. To help our students understand and accept the fact that God doesn't want them to wait—he wants them to begin living for him now
2. To help our students think about and begin to grasp what God's mission(s) for each of them is right now

What You'll Need

Bibles

Paper

Pens or pencils

Notebooks or paper for your students to write on

Whiteboard or chalkboard (optional)

Group Discussion

Review

Get your group talking about some of the big ideas you've covered in this six-week study as a way of preparing them to think about accepting the mission God has for them right now.

Introduce this discussion by saying something like the following in your own words:

For the last five weeks, we've been asking ourselves the questions, *Why not now? Why should we wait any longer to take God seriously? Why shouldn't we expect to do hard things for him? Why shouldn't we expect him to use us to do things that matter? What are we waiting for?*

Let's talk about some of those big ideas. (Use any of the questions below you think might be helpful.)

Do you think people your age are too young to do risky things? What's the difference between taking smart risks and dumb risks?

Does God want you to take risks? What kinds of risks does he expect you to take?

Are people your age too young to say no to real temptation to sin? Should we just expect that if you face hard temptations, you'll automatically give in?

How does God help us face temptation and walk away without giving in? What does saying no to temptation cost us? Are you too young to be expected to pay that price?

Are people your age too young to be brave—too young to walk into dangerous situations to do the right thing? Are you too young to make a clear-minded choice to face danger for the good of others?

Does God care if you're brave or not? What does trusting God have to do with being brave?

Are people your age too young to need wisdom? Do your choices really matter? Do they have real consequences?

Does God give wisdom to students? How do we get wisdom?

Should we expect people your age to go along with the crowd all the time? Should we expect that peer pressure is too hard to overcome and that you can't help yourself from giving in to do wrong things?

How can someone live and excel right in the middle of their culture without going along with the crowd into sinful choices? How can students stand stronger for their convictions?

After you've finished the review of what you've learned during the past five weeks, say to your students (in your own words):

Today we're going to talk about a teenage girl who was given a very specific and difficult mission from God, and we're going to pay attention to how she was able to say yes. Then we're going to think about what God's asking us to do in our world right now.

Bible Study

Backstory

Explain to your group that you know they've heard the story of the angel's visit to Mary many times before—usually at Christmas. In fact, some of them may have played Mary—or the angel—on stage for a Christmas production once or twice.

Ask them to try to look at the story with fresh eyes today—to try not to think of it as a Christmas story:

Mary was a small-town girl, very probably a teenager. It was common at this time in history for older men in their twenties or thirties, once they were established in some kind of a career, to make arrangements with a family to marry one of their teenage daughters. Joseph had likely done that with Mary's father. Mary would have been considered an adult in her culture, ready to take on the role of wife, mother, and homemaker.

We don't know how far in the future her wedding was scheduled, but we do know that Mary had never had sex with anyone, including her fiancé Joseph. Jewish girls who took their religion seriously were very, very careful about avoiding even the appearance of sexual activity before they were married.

And, based on Mary's responses in the story, we know she took her faith in God seriously. She knew the Scriptures. She'd been raised to trust God. And God was going to ask her to do a very difficult thing.

Scripture: Luke 1:26-55

The Big Question: What can we learn from Mary's story about accepting the mission God gives us?

1. Mary Was Favored by God to Do a Hard Thing

Ask a student to read Luke 1:26-28 out loud to the group. Emphasize the following in your own words:

Before the angel said anything else to Mary about her mission, he told her that she was highly favored and God was with her.

Sometimes we're tempted to believe that God asks us to do things for him as a punishment or that he's a harsh master ordering around his servants. We see God's instructions to us as a burden.

That's a lie that keeps us from enjoying the missions he gives us. The truth is that God loves us deeply. The Bible tells us that he chose us to be in his family even before he created the world, that he lovingly put us together in our mothers' bodies, and that he's always aware of what's going on with us—even down to the number of hairs on our heads.

When God asks us, then, to do a hard thing—to accept a difficult mission—he only does it because he favors us. He knows we can do anything with his help, through Jesus.

What better way could we possibly hope to spend our lives than to be used by God to accomplish his plan for the universe?

God asked Mary to do a hard thing because he favored her. He favors you too, and he's always with you through Jesus.

2. Mary Asked, "How?" Not, "Why Me?"

Ask another student to read Luke 1:29-37 out loud.

Mary was freaked out, but she kept her cool. The angel encouraged her not to be afraid and then told her again that being given this mission from God meant that God favored her.

Then he told her what was going to happen. She would get pregnant with the Son of God. She would carry and give birth to the Messiah, and he would make everything right.

First, notice that the angel didn't scold Mary for being afraid. Fear's a normal human reaction. Sometimes we freak out a little when we think about doing what God asks us to do. That's okay as long as we don't cling to the fear and let it keep us from accepting the mission.

Second, Mary didn't just quietly wait for the angel to go away. She didn't really understand what he was saying. How could she? Nobody had ever become pregnant without having sex before. She didn't get it. So she asked a "how" question.

Sometimes, we're afraid to tell God we don't understand what he wants us to do. There's nothing wrong with saying to him, "I don't get it. Help me to understand." That shows that we believe God—not that we don't.

Mary didn't say, "Why me?" She didn't challenge God's choice for her. She just asked for more information.

It's always okay for us to ask and then go looking for help to understand the mission God's called us to do.

3. Mary Accepted the Mission as a Servant, Not a Hero

Ask a third student to read out loud to the group, this time from Luke 1:38.

Of course, we know Mary said yes to the mission. In fact, it's not clear that she even had a choice. The angel simply told her, "This will happen to you."

Still, Mary accepted the mission—and she did so with the attitude of a servant.

We don't have many servants in our culture. We have employees—people who're paid to do a job and are only expected to do what they get paid to do. We've seen servants, though, in stories and in other cultures. We know that a servant's job in life is to do whatever the master tells him or her to do. The purpose of a servant is to help another person accomplish his or her plans.

Mary saw herself as "the Lord's servant." She would do what she was asked.

We sometimes make the mistake of accepting a mission and then making it all about us. We think that being given the mission makes us the hero of the story. We can become proud and arrogant even while we're doing what God has told us to do.

Mary understood this was still God's story—she was just given a role to play in it.

4. Mary Shared Her Mission and Was Affirmed

Have someone else read Luke 1:39-45 to the group.

The first thing Mary did after accepting the mission was to rush to talk about it with someone who'd had a similar experience. The angel had told her that her older cousin Elizabeth was also carrying a miracle baby. Mary wanted to tell someone that she'd accepted a mission from God.

This is a huge step that we often skip. We know that God loves us and has given us meaningful things to do in the world. We make a private decision to follow Jesus in some specific way, maybe after hearing a sermon or going to a retreat. But then we try to act on it without telling anyone.

If you've accepted God's mission for your life, find someone to tell. Talk to another believer who also takes God's instructions to him or her seriously. Explain what you've been thinking about, what you plan to do in your life right now for God in Christ.

And then listen.

In Mary's case, she didn't say anything to Elizabeth except, "Hi." Before Mary could say anything else, God filled Elizabeth in on all the details through the Holy Spirit and the bouncing baby inside of her. How big of a deal that must have been for Mary to hear from another person the confirmation that what the angel said to her was true.

It'll be huge for you too, to hear another Christian say to you, "I'm so excited for you. You're on the right path. You couldn't do anything better with your life than to follow where God's leading you right now."

5. Mary Believed and Praised Her Strong God

Another reader can take the group through Mary's song in Luke 1:46-55.

Elizabeth said this to Mary: "Blessed is she who has believed that the Lord would fulfill his promises to her!"

Mary isn't praised because she was so great at the mission God gave to her. She wasn't praised for taking all her vitamins, getting plenty of rest, and keeping the baby inside of her safe. She wasn't praised for being really good at being pregnant.

Mary was praised by Elizabeth (and God's Word) for believing that God would do what he said.

That's really the test of your mission, too. It's not about how well you can accomplish what God gives you; it's about whether you'll trust him.

Mary got that and responded with this song. She praised God. She stayed humble by giving him all of the credit for accomplishing his plan through her.

When we choose to keep praising God in the middle of doing what he's given us to do, it'll help us to keep going, to remember that it's his mission and he always keeps his promises.

Activity/Group Discussion

What's Your Mission?

Make sure everyone in the room has paper and something to write with. It may also be helpful for you to have a whiteboard, chalkboard, or some other way of writing things down for all to see.

Explain the following in your own words:

We've talked a lot today about how to accept your mission. Now it's time to talk about what God's mission for you is. What has he specifically asked you to do?

I'm here to tell you that God has shown me at least three things he wants you to do for him with your life right now. I'm going to tell you what those three things are and then give you the chance to come up with a few more. Get ready to write these down.

1. **God's mission for you is to let the world see Christ in you.**

   Mary's mission was to carry Christ inside of her. God used her ability to do that to bring Jesus into the world and accomplish his plan for all of us.

   God showed me he has a mission like that for you—to show Jesus to the world by letting everyone see him in you. Let me read to you the words he said to me: "God has chosen to make known among the Gentiles the glorious riches of this mystery, which is Christ in you, the hope of glory." (Colossians 1:27)

Okay, yes, that's a verse from the Bible. And, yes, God did show that to me when I read it. That's one way he gives us our missions. Here's another mission he's given to you:

2. **God's mission for you is to use what he's given you to serve other Christians.**

This is absolutely what God wants you to do with your life. Several passages in the Bible tell us that every Christian is given at least one very powerful gift from God to use specifically to serve other believers. (Check out 1 Corinthians 12.) God didn't send an angel to tell you that; he sent you the message in the Bible, instead. But it's no less true. That's what you are meant to do.

3. **God's mission for you is to be kind to everyone.**

Does that sound like a stupid mission? I didn't make it up. Ephesians 4:32 is really clear: "Be kind and compassionate to one another."

The point I'm making is that the Bible is full of specific missions God has for you to accomplish right now in your life. Each mission matters. Each one is important. Each one is for you.

Group Discussion

Your Specific Mission

In a minute we'll also talk about what kind of specific mission God might have for you that isn't written in the Bible. First, though, let's come up with a few other instructions from God, missions he's given to each of us that matter today.

Ask your group to suggest other instructions from God in the Bible that are specific to their lives right now. As they do, write them down for all to see, and encourage them to write them down as well. If you need to help, suggestions could include obeying parents, forgiving as God has forgiven us, telling people about Jesus, etc. Try to limit these "missions" to positive commands, rather than instructions *not* to do something.

Now let's talk about what specific missions God might have just for you.

Recap with Paul's Story

You might be thinking that I cheated a little bit in telling you that God's mission for your life is to do the things he's told us in the Bible to do. I don't think I am. I think that's the reason he gave the Bible to us: to help us to know how he wants us to live.

But it's also true that God sometimes gives to us missions specifically for us. That's what he did with Mary. He also gave Paul a specific mission:

> And for this purpose I was appointed a herald and an apostle—I am telling the truth, I am not lying—and a true and faithful teacher of the Gentiles. (1 Timothy 2:7)

God told Paul that his job in the world was to tell all the non-Jewish people about Jesus. It was a hard job. Many people hated Paul for it. He was beaten, stoned, shipwrecked, and eventually killed for doing the job God gave him to do.

But Paul accepted the mission in some ways that were similar to Mary:

1. Paul understood that God gave him the mission because God favored him.
2. Paul asked lots of "how" questions but rejected the self-pity of "why me?"
3. Paul often called himself the Lord's servant (or even slave). He knew he wasn't the hero of the story.
4. After he was given the mission, Paul met with the others who'd been given similar missions, and they affirmed his mission, too.
5. Paul kept believing God and kept praising God for keeping his promises.

God has a very specific mission, or set of missions, for each of us as well. Often, we don't know what they are until we find ourselves doing them. Your mission for a day might simply be to encourage one specific person. Your mission in life might be to become a missionary to France, or it might be to become a nuclear physicist for God's glory, or it might be to spend a year in a hospital ministering to a nursing staff while you're recovering from a terrible accident.

The question for each day is, *Will you accept the mission?* Will you answer God's call to do what he's given you to do wherever it leads you?

Conclusion Story

Wrap up the lesson by telling your class the story of Zach Hunter:

When Zach Hunter was just twelve years old, he learned that there were twenty-seven million slaves in the world. He felt sad and angry and wanted to do something about it. He started a campaign called Loose Change to Loosen Chains (ijm.org/get-involved/youth), and he involved other kids and teenagers in asking people to donate their spare change to the cause of rescuing people from slavery. The money would go to support the International Justice Mission and other groups actively seeking an end to slavery.

Here's the deal, though: When Zach started all of this, he was just a shy, sometimes nervous kid who didn't have a lot of confidence. Since then, Zach has helped to raise huge sums of money and has written three books about the causes he's passionate about. He speaks all over the country.

God had a mission for Zach to help people escape from slavery—even though Zach was "just" a student—and Zach accepted that mission.

There was another man in history whom God used to help bring an end to slavery. His name was William Wilberforce, and he too was convinced that God had given him that mission. Zach recently tweeted this quote from Wilberforce: "God Almighty has set before me two great objects, the suppression of the Slave Trade and the Reformation of Manners."

What mission is God giving you today? Right now? Have you made the mistake of thinking you can't do anything that really matters until you're older? Have you made the mistake of thinking you're too shy, or not smart enough, or not spiritual enough, or too busy to do what God wants you to do?

Why wait? Why not decide *right now* to accept God's missions for you, whatever they are, no matter how risky or hard they may be? What could you possibly do with your life that would matter more?

Closing Prayer

Close your session in prayer. Thank God for all the gifts, talents, abilities, and opportunities he's given to you and your students. Ask him to make it very clear to all of you what he wants you to do with your lives this week. And then ask him to give each of you the courage to accept the mission, no matter how hard it might be.

Following Up

Do you want to reinforce the main points of this session with your group during the week? Here are a few things you could send out via Facebook, text, Twitter, or email.

Note: Don't send them all. It's helpful to send one the day after your group meets, and then maybe send another a couple of days later.

Session Reinforcement

Are you on a mission from God, or are you just killing time today? What are you going to do next?

Quick: What are three hard things God wants you to do today?

Whose story are you living in, yours or God's? Are you the servant or the hero?

Why does it matter how you live today?

Of course, these are just starter ideas. Customize these to fit your own group, group name, audience, etc.—or just write something way better!

notes

session 1

1. Caroline Black, "Cheerleader Kealey Oliver to the Rescue: 16-Year-Old Tackles Would-Be Thief at Mall," CBS News, July 28, 2010, http://www.cbsnews.com/8301-504083_162-20011925-504083.html.

session 2

1. Jennifer H. Pfeifer et al., "Entering Adolescence: Resistance to Peer Influence, Risky Behavior, and Neural Changes in Emotion Reactivity," *Neuron* 69 (2011): 1029–1036.

session 4

1. J. D. Rucker, "Teen Trades up on Craigslist from Phone to Porsche in 2 Years," *Auto in the News*, July 20, 2010, http://www.autoin thenews.com/teen-trades-up-on-craigslist-from-phone-to-porsche-in-2-years/.

Share Your Thoughts

With the Author: Your comments will be forwarded to the author when you send them to *zauthor@zondervan.com*.

With Zondervan: Submit your review of this book by writing to *zreview@zondervan.com*.

Free Online Resources at
www.zondervan.com

Zondervan AuthorTracker: Be notified whenever your favorite authors publish new books, go on tour, or post an update about what's happening in their lives at www.zondervan.com/authortracker.

Daily Bible Verses and Devotions: Enrich your life with daily Bible verses or devotions that help you start every morning focused on God. Visit www.zondervan.com/newsletters.

Free Email Publications: Sign up for newsletters on Christian living, academic resources, church ministry, fiction, children's resources, and more. Visit www.zondervan.com/newsletters.

Zondervan Bible Search: Find and compare Bible passages in a variety of translations at www.zondervanbiblesearch.com.

Other Benefits: Register yourself to receive online benefits like coupons and special offers, or to participate in research.

ZONDERVAN®

ZONDERVAN.com/
AUTHORTRACKER
follow your favorite authors